CHAIRMAN
RICHARD POULTER

PUBLISHER
NICK POULTER

EDITOR
SIMON ARRON

WRITTEN BY
SIMON ARRON & TONY DODGINS

ART EDITOR
RYAN BAPTISTE

RESULTS & DATA
DAVID HAYHOE

DIRECTOR
STEVEN PALMER

PUBLISHING DEVELOPMENT MANAGER
PETER MERCER

SALES PROMOTION
ANNALISA ZANELLA

PHOTOGRAPHY
LAT PHOTOGRAPHIC & MARTYN ELFORD

GRAPHICS
RUSSELL LEWIS

ALL RESULTS AND DATA
© FIA 2002

GRAND PRIX YEAR
is published by
Hazleton Publishing Ltd.
3 Richmond Hill
Richmond, Surrey
TW10 6RE, England

**Colour reproduction and Printing by
The Core Group Ltd, Newbury**

**© Hazleton Publishing Ltd. 2002
is part of the Profile Media Group PLC**

ISBN: 1 903135 16 8

www.hazletonpublishing.com

DISTRIBUTORS

UNITED KINGDOM
Haynes Publishing
Sparkford
Nr Yeovil
Somerset
BA22 7JJ
Tel: 01963 440635
Fax: 01963 440001

NORTH AMERICA
Motorbooks International
PO Box 1
729 Prospect Ave.
Osceola
Wisconsin 54020, USA
Tel: (1) 715 294 3345
Fax: (1) 715 294 4448

REST OF THE WORLD
Menoshire Ltd
Unit 13
21 Wadsworth Road
Perivale
Middlesex UB6 7LQ
Tel: 020 8566 7344
Fax: 020 8991 2439

2002 FIA FORMULA ONE WORLD CHAMPIONSHIP

FEATURES

FOREWORD BY MURRAY WALKER

WHEN PEOPLE ASK ME TO NOMINATE GREAT MOTOR racing performances it is usually a question of selecting individual events. In the light of recent history, however, it will be tempting in future to single out the whole of the 2002 season for special mention.

There have been feats of dominance in the past – by Alberto Ascari in the early 1950s, Jim Clark in 1963, McLaren in 1988 and Nigel Mansell in 1992, to name but a few – but there has never been anything to match the level of Michael Schumacher's supremacy during the season just past.

Some say it has made the racing predictable: I would counter that it has been a privilege to watch an extraordinary sportsman at the peak of his powers. People used to pay good money to see Björn Borg, Muhammad Ali, George Best or Donald Bradman tear rivals apart in their respective fields, just as they do today to watch Tiger Woods, Sachin Tendulkar and, yes, Schumacher.

Even by the German's lofty, record-breaking standards this was an extraordinary campaign: 11 wins, 144 points (an average of 8.47 per race from a maximum 10), a 100 per cent reliability record and he never finished lower than third... some tally. It is more than 10 years since he scored his first win – and in that light his unquenchable appetite for racing is even more remarkable. Comparisons between leading drivers of different eras are tenuous, but Schumacher's place in the sport's pantheon of greats is undeniable.

It might have been a one-sided season but there were several memorable side issues: the confirmation of Kimi Räikkönen's flamboyant speed; Juan Pablo Montoya's absolute mastery of the qualifying lap; the re-emergence of Jenson Button; David Coulthard's marvellous Monaco triumph and Toyota's arrival among the motor racing elite.

Whatever you thought about 2002, *Grand Prix Year* has all the key issues covered in its traditionally refreshing style. It's a colourful companion to help you while away the winter months as you wait for an answer to F1's big question: can anybody peg back Ferrari? It will be fascinating to watch them try.

Here's to 2003.

THE CLASS OF 2002

SCUDERIA FERRARI MARLBORO
FERRARI F2002-FERRARI V10

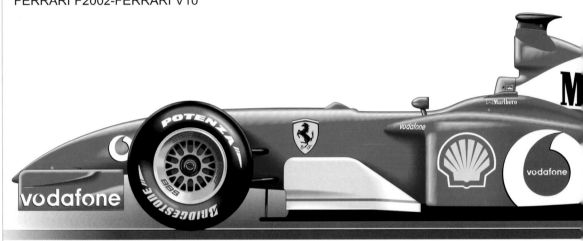

WEST McLAREN MERCEDES
McLAREN MP4-17-MERCEDES V10

DRIVERS
3 DAVID COULTHARD (GBR)
4 KIMI RÄIKKÖNEN (FIN)
TEST TEAM
ALEXANDER WURZ (AUT)
TEAM PRINCIPAL
RON DENNIS (GBR)
IF TEAMS WERE BISCUITS THIS ONE WOULD BE
A Cadbury's Finger – been around for ages, stylish but functional, a hint of the avant-garde (especially the white chocolate variety)

IN A NUTSHELL
After a record-breaking six years as team-mates, the Mika Häkkinen/David Coulthard axis was finally broken because the Finn decided he would prefer to worry about changing nappies rather than gear clusters. In nine seasons of F1 racing, this was DC's first as the most experienced driver on a team's books. In Mika's place came Kimi Räikkönen. The difference between them? Four letters on the side of the cockpit but nothing in terms of speed

JUST AS FOOTBALL FANS HAVE HOPE IN THEIR HEARTS WHEN A NEW SEASON BEGINS IN AUGUST (UNLESS THEY SUPPORT BRISTOL ROVERS), SO FORMULA ONE TEAMS HAVE A SPRING IN THEIR STEP AS MARCH APPROACHES AND THEY PREPARE TO SPEND MORE THAN 20 HOURS IN A CRAMPED METAL TUBE EN ROUTE TO MELBOURNE. AT LEAST, SOME OF THEM DO. HERE'S YOUR AT-A-GLANCE GUIDE TO THE KEY CHARACTERS AND. MARCEL LASSÉE

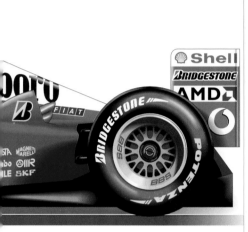

DRIVERS
1 MICHAEL SCHUMACHER (GER)
2 RUBENS BARRICHELLO (BRA)
TEST TEAM
LUCA BADOER (ITA) LUCIANO BURTI (BRA)
TEAM PRINCIPAL
JEAN TODT (FRA)
IF TEAMS WERE BISCUITS THIS ONE WOULD BE
A Kit-Kat – wrapped in red and hard to beat at any time of the day

IN A NUTSHELL
Having failed to win any kind of F1 title between 1983 and 1999, Ferrari began 2002 looking for its third straight success in the championship for drivers and a fourth in that for constructors. In its favour? Best driver, best car, two test drivers, vast resources, excellent coffee machine in its motorhome. Weak points? Have spent seven months thinking about that one and haven't come up with anything yet

BMW WILLIAMSF1 TEAM
WILLIAMS FW24-BMW V10

DRIVERS
5 RALF SCHUMACHER (GER)
6 JUAN PABLO MONTOYA (COL)
TEST TEAM
ANTONIO PIZZONIA (BRA)
MARC GENÉ (ESP)
TEAM PRINCIPAL
SIR FRANK WILLIAMS (GBR)
IF TEAMS WERE BISCUITS THIS ONE WOULD BE
A caramel wafer – looked to have all the right ingredients but ultimately not quite as good as it looks or sounds

IN A NUTSHELL
The previous season's FW23 chassis offered a solid platform from which to develop, but its successor looked like little more than a mild update – largely because that's exactly what it was. Main rivals Ferrari and McLaren were far more adventurous during the off-season. Much was expected of Juan Pablo Montoya now that he had a year of experience under his belt, while Schuey Jnr provided a solid, less spectacular foil. George Best and Nobby Stiles, in essence

SAUBER PETRONAS
SAUBER C21-PETRONAS V10

DRIVERS
7 NICK HEIDFELD (GER)
8 FELIPE MASSA (BRA)
8 HEINZ-HARALD FRENTZEN (GER), right
TEST TEAM NONE the car was built for drivers who could equally have made it as flat jockeys and most others who tried to get in didn't fit
TEAM PRINCIPAL
PETER SAUBER (SUI)
IF TEAMS WERE BISCUITS THIS ONE WOULD BE
A McVities Digestive – simple but elegant, plenty of substance, better than you might expect

IN A NUTSHELL
Halfway through the season Nick Heidfeld summed it up: "I'm never going to challenge for the world championship while I'm here," he said, "but this is a great little team." Fact: compact, well-drilled outfit using customer engines has been making many of its manufacturer-backed rivals look like a bunch of chimps – despite being based out on a limb in Switzerland, where circuit racing has been banned for 47 years

DHL JORDAN HONDA
JORDAN EJ12-HONDA V10

DRIVERS
9 GIANCARLO FISICHELLA (ITA)
10 TAKUMA SATO (JAP)
TEST TEAM
MARCEL LASSÉE (GER)
TEAM PRINCIPAL
EDDIE JORDAN (IRL)
IF TEAMS WERE BISCUITS THIS ONE WOULD BE
A Jaffa Cake – neat and well presented, bit of a hard edge but fun at heart

IN A NUTSHELL
Fisichella is one of the best in the business. Sato is one of the most promising rookies and the finest prospect yet to have emerged from the Far East (although the Japanese had hardly heard of him because he did most of his formative racing in Europe). On the minus side, however, it had more human than financial resources and by mid-season about 40 staff had to be laid off. It managed to regroup, however, with barely a ripple in its (admittedly modest) performance curve

LUCKY STRIKE BAR HONDA
BAR 004-HONDA V10

DRIVERS
11 JACQUES VILLENEUVE (CAN)
12 OLIVIER PANIS (FRA)
TEST TEAM
ANTHONY DAVIDSON (GBR) RYO FUKUDA (JAP)
PATRICK LEMARIÉ (FRA)
TEAM PRINCIPAL DAVID RICHARDS (GBR)
IF TEAMS WERE BISCUITS THIS ONE WOULD BE
Formerly the small, digestive-style thing that always got left until last in the Christmas selection box, because its brash arrival in 1999 put everybody off. Has since assumed Custard Cream standards of all-round popularity within the paddock, however

IN A NUTSHELL
Fourth season in F1 – but its first under new management. Incoming boss David Richards was world champion rally co-driver in 1981, has enjoyed colossal success with a variety of manufacturers including Subaru (World Rally Championship), BMW and Alfa Romeo (British Touring Car Championship) and is credited with organising the emergence of rallying as a mainstream TV sport. Next job: sort this lot out. Arrival of new technical director Geoff Willis from Williams a good starting point

MILD SEVEN RENAULT F1 TEAM
RENAULT R202-RENAULT V10

DRIVERS
14 JARNO TRULLI (ITA)
15 JENSON BUTTON (GBR)
TEST TEAM
FERNANDO ALONSO (ESP)
TEAM PRINCIPALS
FLAVIO BRIATORE (ITA) JEAN-JACQUES HIS (FRA)
IF TEAMS WERE BISCUITS THIS ONE WOULD BE
A Café Noir – right at the cutting edge in terms of taste and slightly-avant-garde, but prone to having bits break off

IN A NUTSHELL
Back in Formula One as a complete entity for the first time since 1985, although physically little had changed since the previous season, the team's last under the Benetton label. The chassis shop remained in Oxfordshire, the engine plant in Paris. The name might have changed, however, but the familiar colour scheme meant that everybody was still calling them Benettons until well into the season. Jenson Button came into 2002 much more focused. Jarno Trulli was the same as ever: overtaking remained an alien science, until he got to Monza

JAGUAR RACING
JAGUAR R3-FORD COSWORTH V10

DRIVERS
16 EDDIE IRVINE (GBR)
17 PEDRO DE LA ROSA (ESP)
TEST TEAM JAMES COURTNEY (AUS)
ANDRÉ LOTTERER (BEL)
TEAM PRINCIPAL
NIKI LAUDA (AUT)
IF TEAMS WERE BISCUITS THIS ONE WOULD BE
A chocolate Yoyo – promising on the surface but likely to leave you in a bit of a mess

IN A NUTSHELL
"It's lighter, the aerodynamics are better, everything's better. It has to be a big step forward over the R2." The words of Eddie Irvine at the launch of Jaguar's all-new R3. Then he drove it... and suggested that perhaps the team would be better off sticking with the R2 after all. The season turned into what was effectively an eight-month test session for the team that has been getting through technical directors at about the same rate as children eat packets of crisps. Eventually there were signs of progress, although Niki Lauda still hasn't learned how to tuck his shirt in

ORANGE ARROWS
ARROWS A23-ASIATECH V10

DRIVERS
20 HEINZ-HARALD FRENTZEN (GER)
21 ENRIQUE BERNOLDI (BRA)
TEST TEAM Be nice to have one, but if you can't afford to attend all the races it would be a touch extravagant to do anything in-between times
TEAM PRINCIPAL
TOM WALKINSHAW (GBR)
IF TEAMS WERE BISCUITS THIS ONE WOULD BE
An Abbey Crunch dunked in tea – initially delicious, but likely to disappear irretrievably into the bottom of the cup before you've finished

IN A NUTSHELL
Neat, effective chassis. Strong engine (ideal for embarrassing Jaguar on a regular basis). Experienced, still-hungry team leader in Frentzen. Quickish (but, more importantly, well connected) number two in Bernoldi. If only they could have found the backing to mix all the components effectively this could have been a very good campaign. Instead it turned into a half-season whose fleeting promise was quickly forgotten beneath a mountain of rising debts and protracted sales negotiations

KL MINARDI ASIATECH
MINARDI PS02-EUROPEAN V10

DRIVERS
22 ALEX YOONG (MAL)
23 MARK WEBBER (AUS)
22 ANTHONY DAVIDSON (GBR)
TEST TEAM
DAVID SAELENS (BEL)
TEAM PRINCIPAL
PAUL STODDART (AUS)

IF TEAMS WERE BISCUITS THIS ONE WOULD BE
A Rich Tea – no frills, but really rather good

IN A NUTSHELL
Perennial tail-ender started the year with a sharper edge, a greater sense of organisation than it has known for some time and a definite rising star in Webber. It also had a couple of compromises: Yoong's handy stock of Malaysian backers was offset by his lack of experience at this level (which ultimately led to him taking a two-race summer break, to collect his thoughts); and there were those in the team who said Asiatech's V10 engines had barely changed since they used to have the word "Peugeot" stamped on the cam covers a couple of years beforehand. Still, at least they didn't break down very often

PANASONIC TOYOTA RACING
TOYOTA TF 102-TOYOTA RVX-02 V10

DRIVERS
24 MIKA SALO (FIN)
25 ALLAN McNISH (GBR)
TEST TEAM
RYAN BRISCOE (AUS)
STÉPHANE SARRAZIN (FRA)
TEAM PRINCIPAL
OVE ANDERSSON (SWE)

IF TEAMS WERE BISCUITS THIS ONE WOULD BE
One of those huge choc-chip cookies your local newsagent sells – promising after a couple of nibbles but ultimately too dense and stodgy

IN A NUTSHELL
New kids on the block. Colossal budget. Vast amount of individual experience, but yet to gel as a unit. Such was the level of its preparation that it had completed a full dummy race weekend the previous year in Austria. This included having the drivers attend press conferences in an empty media room. Such attention to detail helped the team make a brighter start than had been anticipated, although fortunes subsequently waned. Then some faceless suit in a boardroom decided it would be a good idea to pitch both drivers for 2003 just when the team was crying out for stability and continuity

11

DRIVER	NATIONALITY	BORN
RUBENS BARRICHELLO	(BRA)	MAY 23 1972
ENRIQUE BERNOLDI	**(BRA)**	**OCT 19 1978**
JENSON BUTTON	(GBR)	JAN 18 1980
DAVID COULTHARD	**(GBR)**	**MAR 27 1971**
ANTHONY DAVIDSON	(GBR)	APR 18 1979
PEDRO DE LA ROSA	**(ESP)**	**FEB 24 1971**
GIANCARLO FISICHELLA	(ITA)	JAN 14 1973
HEINZ-HARALD FRENTZEN	**(GER)**	**MAY 18 1967**
NICK HEIDFELD	(GER)	MAY 10 1977
EDDIE IRVINE	**(GBR)**	**NOV 10 1965**
FELIPE MASSA	(BRA)	APR 25 1981
ALLAN McNISH	**(GBR)**	**DEC 29 1969**
JUAN PABLO MONTOYA	(COL)	SEP 20 1975
OLIVIER PANIS	**(FRA)**	**SEP 2 1966**
KIMI RÄIKKÖNEN	(FIN)	OCT 17 1979
MIKA SALO	**(FIN)**	**NOV 30 1966**
TAKUMA SATO	(JAP)	JAN 28 1977
MICHAEL SCHUMACHER	**(GER)**	**JAN 3 1969**
RALF SCHUMACHER	(GER)	JUN 20 1975
JARNO TRULLI	**(ITA)**	**JUL 13 1974**
JACQUES VILLENEUVE	(CDN)	APR 9 1971
MARK WEBBER	**(AUS)**	**AUG 27 1976**
ALEX YOONG	(MAL)	JUL 20 1976

THIS YEAR'S PACE ATTACK

THE AVERAGE BAR STOOL IS AS GOOD A PLACE FOR A DEBATE AS THE TURN ONE BRAKING ZONE. TO HELP RESOLVE FROTHY ARGUMENTS, WELCOME TO OUR GUIDE TO A BUNCH OF PEOPLE MOSTLY TOO YOUNG TO REMEMBER THE FORD CORSAIR 2000E. OR SLADE. OR STOKE CITY WINNING THE LEAGUE CUP

RST GRAND PRIX	TOTAL STARTS	WINS	POLES	POINTS SCORED
UTH AFRICA 1993, JORDAN	164	5	6	272
STRALIA 2001, ARROWS	28	0	0	0
STRALIA 2000, WILLIAMS	51	0	0	28
AIN 1994, WILLIAMS	141	12	12	400
NGARY 2002, MINARDI	2	0	0	0
STRALIA 1999, ARROWS	63	0	0	6
STRALIA 1996, MINARDI	107	0	1	82
AZIL 1994, SAUBER	141	3	2	161
STRALIA 2000, PROST	50	0	0	19
PAN 1993, JORDAN	146	4	0	191
STRALIA 2002, SAUBER	16	0	0	4
STRALIA 2002, TOYOTA	16	0	0	0
STRALIA 2001, WILLIAMS	34	1	10	81
AZIL 1994, LIGIER	125	1	0	64
STRALIA 2001, SAUBER	34	0	0	33
PAN 1994, LOTUS	110	0	0	33
STRALIA 2002, JORDAN	17	0	0	2
LGIUM 1991, JORDAN	179	64	50	945
STRALIA 1997, JORDAN	100	4	1	177
STRALIA 1997, MINARDI	97	0	0	38
STRALIA 1996, WILLIAMS	116	11	13	213
STRALIA 2002, MINARDI	16	0	0	2
LY 2001, MINARDI	14	0	0	0

FOSTER'S AUSTRALIAN GRAND PRIX

MICHAEL SCHUMACHER WINS FORMULA ONE RACE. PRETTY CONVENTIONAL AS HEADLINES GO, ALTHOUGH THE OPENING RACE OF THE 2002 CAMPAIGN WAS ANYTHING BUT

HERR DISPLAY: Here, Ralf, watch out for that Ferr... On second thoughts, forget it. Schuey Jnr sets off the chain of events that will decimate the field (above), while, from the left, Montoya, Schuey Snr and some miserable-looking Finnish bloke soak up the post-race plaudits

THE WAY SOME PEOPLE WERE TALKING, YOU COULD BE forgiven for thinking Ferrari had decided to level the playing field by giving Michael Schumacher an Austin Maxi to race in Australia.

True, the Italian team had decided to start the season with its old car, but that was hardly a handicap. It simply built up a fresh batch of F2001 chassis, the same as those Michael had used to dominate the previous season's championship and known to be absolutely bullet-proof (unless Rubens Barrichello's name happens to be painted on the side).

New F1 designs tend to have slightly suspect reliability during the genesis of their careers. Ferrari's latest F2002 looked extremely promising, but the team reckoned its proven chassis would be a safer bet for the opening two races because engineering defects can be tricky to rectify when you are far from home.

Good call.

Everything else that rolled out of a packing crate in Melbourne was pretty much new, but none of it was a match for the outgoing Ferrari. And Schumacher had already indicated that the incoming F2002 chassis would be a major step forward when it was declared race-ready. The future appeared ominously red.

It was Barrichello, however, who beat his team-mate to pole position. Customarily it is baking hot in Melbourne, but a combination of factors – including raging bush fires elsewhere in the country – had upset weather patterns and there was constant drizzle during the pre-race build-up. Barrichello managed the cleanest lap before conditions deteriorated, but it wasn't to do him much good.

The Brazilian led all the way to the braking zone for the first corner, where third-fastest qualifier Ralf Schumacher wasted an explosive start by forgetting an essential motor racing principle that involves

RALF SCHUMACHER WASTED AN EXPLOSIVE START BY FORGETTING AN ESSENTIAL MOTOR RACING PRINCIPLE THAT INVOLVES BRAKING AND CORNER ENTRY SPEEDS

braking and corner entry speeds. Fearful that there might be some kind of incident, which there often is in Australia due to race-rustiness, Barrichello claimed he braked a little later than usual, but still Ralf steamed into him at colossal speed.

The Williams took off and flew for a frightening distance before landing the right way up in a gravel trap. In the confusion Schuey Snr and Kimi Räikkönen skated across the grass, Giancarlo Fisichella tangled with both Saubers and Olivier Panis, Jenson Button and Allan McNish all ran into various bits of wreckage. So, too, did Mika Salo, but he pitted for a track-rod replacement before rejoining a lap in arrears. Räikkönen also stopped for repairs, although he didn't lose much time. Neither Arrows was involved, largely because its drivers failed to get off the line. After starting late they would both be disqualified, Heinz-Harald Frentzen for ignoring a red light in the pit lane, Enrique Bernoldi for using his spare car when he wasn't supposed to.

The Safety Car came into play for several laps to allow eight wrecks to be swept away, while David Coulthard led a thin train of survivors that comprised Jarno Trulli, Juan Pablo Montoya, Schuey Snr, Eddie Irvine, Pedro de la Rosa, Takuma Sato, Mark Webber, Alex Yoong, Jacques Villeneuve, Kimi Räikkönen and Mika Salo.

Schumacher passed Montoya at the restart when the Colombian ran

WEBBED FEAT

PITS SPECIAL: McLaren's super-quick service (above) gave Räikkönen a whiff of second place – for about 100 metres, at which point he ploughed straight off the track. New Jaguar R3 (below) was bog slow but, happily for Irvine, reliable. Left, nectar also now available in brunette

THE TOP-SELLING F1 SOUVENIRS? EASY. Anywhere you go, the Ferrari motif is in demand.

In Australia, however, the Prancing Horse limped in a poor second in the sales charts – to Minardi. It was suggested that Italy's second F1 team – and F1's 11th – did more merchandising business during Australian GP week than all its rivals combined.

Melbourne's Minardi mania was down to two things. Team principal Paul Stoddart hails from Coburg, a local suburb, and took control of the organisation before the start of the 2001 season. That caused a ripple of interest, but now he had signed rising star Mark Webber from Queanbeyan, New South Wales, to put an Australian on his home GP grid for the first time since David Brabham drove a Simtek in 1994.

Stoddart and Webber (pictured having his intestinal strength put through a pre-race test by the local air force, above) were available to all and sundry before the race – the general public included – and conducted themselves courteously and with good humour.

If you tuned in to a local radio station, you were sure to hear a screaming exhortation: "Can Mark Webber win in Albert Park on Sunday? Come along to see for yourself. There are still a few tickets left."

The obvious answer, of course, was that he couldn't, unless a huge pile-up took out everybody bar the Minardis and perhaps the odd Jaguar.

Ralf Schumacher didn't trigger destruction on quite that scale at the start, but he did enough to give Webber a tilt at Minardi's first top-six finish since the GP of Europe in September 1999. And the 25-year-old didn't waste the chance. He drove beautifully – especially when fending off Mika Salo's late challenge, which only materialised because Webber had been delayed by a refuelling glitch during a routine stop.

Webber and Stoddart were in tears by the end. It's rare to see such genuine emotion in F1. Nice, too.

17

APPOSITE BLOCK: clockwise from top, Montoya holds off Schuey – but it was clear that we were already in for a season of writing captions about the German; McNish's long-overdue F1 debut lasted only seconds; Trulli heads off in the general direction of Sydney

THE JAGUARS WERE INEFFECTIVE ALL WEEKEND, BUT CIRCUMSTANCES ALLOWED IRVINE TO ENJOY AN IMPROBABLY EASY RUN TO FOURTH

wide, but barely had the race settled down than the Safety Car reappeared after Trulli smacked the wall. This promoted Schuey to second, behind Coulthard, and the German took the lead even before the Safety Car peeled in because a faulty gear selector caused the Scot to run wide across the grass. Coulthard continued to run at a reduced pace but transmission problems eventually forced him out.

The race didn't begin in earnest until the lap 12 restart, when Montoya snatched the lead from Schumacher going into Turn One. He was soon holding the Ferrari up, however, and knew it. "It was only going to be a matter of time before I lost out," he said. On lap 17 his strenuous efforts to stay ahead caused him to run wide at the first turn. Schuey was through and away, this time for keeps.

Räikkönen moved through the field and set the race's quickest time on lap 37, just before his scheduled stop. Smart pit work got him back into the race slightly ahead of Montoya, but he immediately ran wide at the first corner and thus had to settle for third.

The Jaguars were ineffective all weekend, but circumstances allowed Irvine to enjoy an improbably easy run to fourth ahead of local hero Webber (see page 17) and the recovering Salo, who spun while challenging for fifth in the closing stages. Even so, sixth was a major boost for Toyota in its first F1 race; Corollas aren't the only reliable thing it makes – a vital asset on a day such as this.

FLASHBACK

October 26 1986. Adelaide, Australia

IN THE DARK, EARLY HOURS BLEARY-EYED BRITS fumbled around their kitchens in the hunt for a tea bag, still not quite compos mentis after their alarm clocks' brusque interruption.

Nigel Mansell mania was still in its fairly formative stages, but much of the country wanted to watch live as that season's closing grand prix from Adelaide unfurled. Our previous world champion had been James Hunt, 10 years earlier, and here was Mansell on the cusp of success. The Williams-Honda star had spent the season trashing double world champion team-mate Nelson Piquet's reputation and led the Brazilian by seven points going into the Australian finale. And his closest adversary Alain Prost (McLaren-TAG turbo) was six adrift.

Mansell won five of the first 15 races and had led more laps than any other driver. The title would justly have been his. He had no need to push, either. For once he could counter his natural attacking instincts and drive at a controlled pace.

On the 64th of 82 laps he was nearly there, running second between Piquet and Prost, but his tyres were looking slightly threadbare. The team was contemplating whether to bring him in for a precautionary change when his left rear exploded at about 180mph in sixth gear.

Keeping off the concrete walls at that speed was a triumph in itself, albeit not quite the kind he had been anticipating. Williams swiftly called in Piquet for a tyre change and Prost took the lead. The Frenchman's fuel gauge told him he wouldn't make the finish, but he did and so retained his title.

Mansell sloped quietly back to the pits; in the UK, we crawled out of our sleeping bags, grabbed some more tea and went off to watch the Formula Ford Festival at Brands Hatch.

BRITAIN'S BEST-SELLING SINGLES… WHEN NIGEL MANSELL'S TYRE WENT BANG	
1 MADONNA	True Blue
2 FIVE STAR	Rain Or Shine
3 COMMUNARDS	Don't Leave Me This Way
4 PAUL SIMON	You Can Call Me Al
5 NICK BERRY	Every Loser Wins

March 3 2002
ALBERT PARK CIRCUIT
MELBOURNE
CIRCUIT LENGTH: 3.295miles / 5.303km

Starting Grid

2 Barrichello
1m25.843s

1 M Schumacher
1m25.848s

5 R Schumacher
1m26.279s

3 Coulthard
1m26.446s

4 Räikkönen
1m27.161s

6 Montoya
1m27.249s

14 Trulli
1m27.710s

9 Fisichella
1m27.869s

8 Massa
1m27.972s

7 Heidfeld
1m28.232s

15 Button
1m28.361s

12 Panis
1m28.381s

11 Villeneuve
1m28.657s

24 Salo
1m29.205s

20 Frentzen
1m29.474s

25 McNish
1m29.636s

21 Bernoldi
1m29.738s

23 Webber
1m30.086s

16 Irvine
1m30.113s

17 de la Rosa
1m30.192s

22 Yoong
1m31.504s

10 Sato
1m53.351s

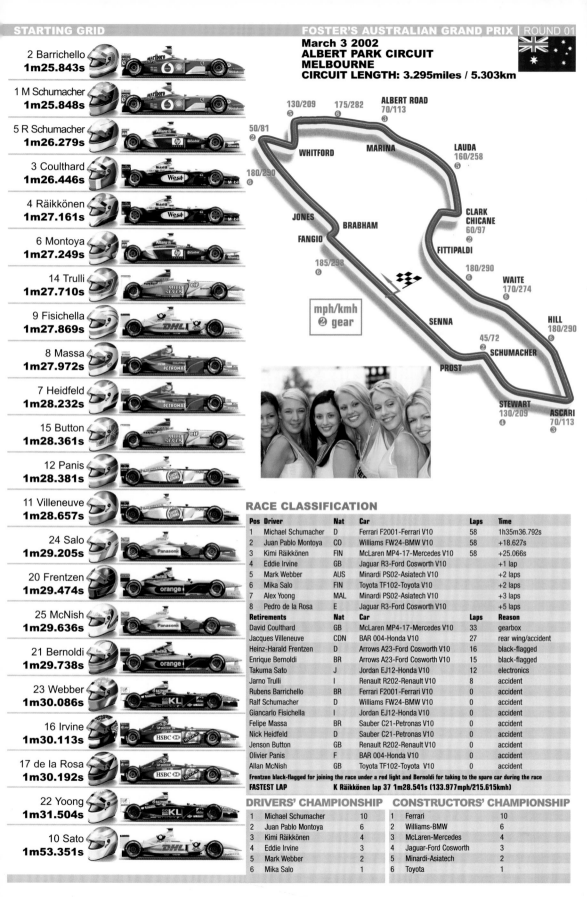

Circuit map — Albert Park Circuit:
ALBERT ROAD 70/113 ③; 130/209 ⑤; 175/282 ⑥; 50/81 ②; WHITFORD; MARINA; LAUDA 160/258 ⑤; 180/290 ⑥; CLARK CHICANE 60/97 ②; JONES; FANGIO; BRABHAM; FITTIPALDI; 185/298 ⑥; 180/290 ⑥; WAITE 170/274 ⑥; HILL 180/290 ⑥; SENNA; PROST; 45/72 ② SCHUMACHER; STEWART 130/209 ④; ASCARI 70/113 ③

mph/kmh ② gear

RACE CLASSIFICATION

Pos	Driver	Nat	Car	Laps	Time
1	Michael Schumacher	D	Ferrari F2001-Ferrari V10	58	1h35m36.792s
2	Juan Pablo Montoya	CO	Williams FW24-BMW V10	58	+18.627s
3	Kimi Räikkönen	FIN	McLaren MP4-17-Mercedes V10	58	+25.066s
4	Eddie Irvine	GB	Jaguar R3-Ford Cosworth V10		+1 lap
5	Mark Webber	AUS	Minardi PS02-Asiatech V10		+2 laps
6	Mika Salo	FIN	Toyota TF102-Toyota V10		+2 laps
7	Alex Yoong	MAL	Minardi PS02-Asiatech V10		+3 laps
8	Pedro de la Rosa	E	Jaguar R3-Ford Cosworth V10		+5 laps

Retirements	Nat	Car	Laps	Reason
David Coulthard	GB	McLaren MP4-17-Mercedes V10	33	gearbox
Jacques Villeneuve	CDN	BAR 004-Honda V10	27	rear wing/accident
Heinz-Harald Frentzen	D	Arrows A23-Ford Cosworth V10	16	black-flagged
Enrique Bernoldi	BR	Arrows A23-Ford Cosworth V10	15	black-flagged
Takuma Sato	J	Jordan EJ12-Honda V10	12	electronics
Jarno Trulli	I	Renault R202-Renault V10	8	accident
Rubens Barrichello	BR	Ferrari F2001-Ferrari V10	0	accident
Ralf Schumacher	D	Williams FW24-BMW V10	0	accident
Giancarlo Fisichella	I	Jordan EJ12-Honda V10	0	accident
Felipe Massa	BR	Sauber C21-Petronas V10	0	accident
Nick Heidfeld	D	Sauber C21-Petronas V10	0	accident
Jenson Button	GB	Renault R202-Renault V10	0	accident
Olivier Panis	F	BAR 004-Honda V10	0	accident
Allan McNish	GB	Toyota TF102-Toyota V10	0	accident

Frentzen black-flagged for joining the race under a red light and Bernoldi for taking to the spare car during the race

FASTEST LAP   K Räikkönen lap 37 1m28.541s (133.977mph/215.615kmh)

DRIVERS' CHAMPIONSHIP

1	Michael Schumacher	10
2	Juan Pablo Montoya	6
3	Kimi Räikkönen	4
4	Eddie Irvine	3
5	Mark Webber	2
6	Mika Salo	1

CONSTRUCTORS' CHAMPIONSHIP

1	Ferrari	10
2	Williams-BMW	6
3	McLaren-Mercedes	4
4	Jaguar-Ford Cosworth	3
5	Minardi-Asiatech	2
6	Toyota	1

FLUX AT THE B.A.R

IN ITS FIRST SEASON UNDER NEW MANAGEMENT, LUCKY STRIKE B.A.R HONDA MADE THE KIND OF PROGRESS THAT AUGURS WELL FOR THE FUTURE. HERE FOLLOWS A PERSPECTIVE ON ITS 2002 CAMPAIGN

TRANSITION IS AN OVER-USED WORD IN SPORT. A football team is usually "in transition" when a new manager fails to arrest a poor run, while the form of a horse is always "transitional" when struggling to bridge a step up in class. The word covers a multitude of spins... but is entirely appropriate to describe Lucky Strike B.A.R Honda in 2002.

For the team, this metamorphosis has been nothing less than positive. Relative to expectations, on-track performances have been generally disappointing – a fact no one at Brackley would try to disguise. But there were genuine signs of improvement and, for the first time since the team's inception in 1998, the blather from B.A.R is now realistic. The reason? Incoming boss David Richards and his new broom.

Richards' shock introduction at the team's car launch in December 2001, as a replacement for founder Craig Pollock, caused a considerable stir. It was F1's biggest pre-season story.

Journalists were also told about Honda's renewed three-year deal with the team, as well as an extended commitment to tyre supplier Bridgestone. Richards said, "I think I can do a lot because the key ingredients are all there. I am most impressed by the honest and open nature of everyone at Lucky Strike B.A.R Honda and, with long-term funding and a qualified engine partner in place, logic says you could be competitive. It's a huge challenge to take on Ferrari, McLaren and Williams but you could aspire to that."

However, while the future looked rosy, Richards and his engineering consultancy Prodrive clearly had a tough task on their hands before they even moved into the hot seat. They had to run with what they had, the BAR004 – in effect the 2001 car with most of its problems ironed out. And that certainly wasn't enough to challenge F1's elite.

Malcolm Oastler, who designed the BAR004, confessed, "We are probably not going to start that strongly." Not exactly waving the white flag before the battle had commenced, but not far off it...

Early portents for the new car weren't particularly promising and the most telling summary was made by Geoffrey Willis, who had been signed from Williams as engineering director during Pollock's reign, although he played no part in the design of the new car. While praising the motivation, skill and enthusiasm he found at Brackley, he would later refer to the BAR004 as "quite good for 1995".

Over the next three months, Richards and his main men at Prodrive embarked on a review of the team's infrastructure and operations and set a financial plan for the future. Trimming a bloated organisation was never going to be an easy job, especially when it put more than 50 people out of work, but F1 is a tough business and DR is a tough businessman. He knew what he wanted and it was deemed necessary for the future prosperity of Lucky Strike B.A.R Honda. Oastler fell victim to Richards' spring-clean and Geoffrey Willis was announced as his successor as technical director.

By the time Richards had completed his review, the season was already under way. The team had travelled to race one in Australia with cautious confidence, but it was clear that if Lucky Strike B.A.R Honda was to retain sixth place in the championship for constructors it could be regarded as a major result.

Rain blighted qualifying at the Albert Park opener, leaving only 20 minutes for drivers to secure their place on the grid. Villeneuve tangled with Coulthard on his quick lap, while Panis' hot one was spoilt by a red flag. Subsequently, 12th and 13th was the best the B.A.R boys could achieve. Come race day, however, it needn't have mattered. The first-corner shunt between Ralf Schumacher and Rubens Barrichello caused chaos down the field and eight drivers were eliminated – including Panis. Villeneuve escaped but a rear wing failure ended his afternoon after 27 laps.

Panis had another dismal weekend in Malaysia, where he qualified 18th after spending most of Saturday in the pit garage, his car immobilised by gearbox problems. Despite a mega start he suffered clutch maladies in the race and was out by lap 10. Team-mate Villeneuve battled valiantly to the end, but eighth place is nowhere for an ex-world champion. Team principal David Richards summed up the feeling in the camp by stating, "We have an enormous mountain to climb and we won't achieve our goals without radical changes." Cue the aforementioned B.A.R cull.

After the traumatic internal events during the build-up to round three in Brazil, it was no surprise that a somewhat subdued atmosphere hung over the team. Unfortunately, there was little to cheer Lucky Strike B.A.R Honda on track. Its worst-ever aggregate qualifying performance left Villeneuve and Panis 15th and 17th on the grid for Sunday. Both gained two places at the start, but that was about as good as it got. Olivier made it a hat trick of DNFs

when a broken gearbox knocked him out on lap 26, while Villeneuve was classified 10th after retiring with three laps to go.

Geoffrey Willis made his first appearance at the business end when the series returned to Europe for the San Marino GP, where Honda introduced some engine tweaks. There was a renewed vigour throughout the team and the drivers responded by achieving the best qualifying performance of the year so far. During the race the car looked more competitive and two brisk pit-stops by chief mechanic Alastair Gibson and company elevated JV to within sight of the points. He eventually finished just shy in seventh. Panis was less fortunate and clocked another DNF.

The following races in Spain, Austria and Monaco were where near as positive and produced no points. In general, Panis was having a better time of it in qualifying than his team-mate, but was still unable to get his car to the finish: seven starts, seven unlucky strikes. Meanwhile, Villeneuve finished seventh in Barcelona but was sensational in Austria, where he illustrated why he remains such a hero to many. Gambling on a two-stop strategy, he soon scythed his way past six cars and then used his American racing experience to take advantage of two Safety Car call-outs to gain track position. Eventually it counted for nothing, because most of the cars ahead were on a more suitable one-stop strategy and his engine blew just before the end anyway, but it was still an example of how F1 can whet the appetite.

Canada was expected to be a turning point for Lucky Strike B.A.R Honda. No change in fortune was immediately apparent, but the genesis of the team's strong end-of-year form could be seen in Montreal. The team unloaded an almost entirely new car that included a lighter gearbox, complete with a revised clutch system and the basis of an entirely new rear suspension. The only mild disappointment was news from Japan that Honda's latest evolution of the RA002E engine wasn't quite ready.

Qualifying went fairly well: JV ninth, OP 11th. In the race Villeneuve continued his wretched home form with another DNF after more gutsy driving in a fuel-heavy car topped up for only one stop. Panis, meanwhile, ended his shocking run of bad fortune by finishing eighth. It felt

VILLENEUVE WAS SENSATIONAL IN AUSTRIA, WHERE HE ILLUSTRATED WHY HE REMAINS SUCH A HERO TO MANY. IT WAS AN EXAMPLE OF HOW F1 CAN WHET THE APPETITE

almost like a podium to the beleaguered Frenchman.

The GP of Europe at the revised Nürburgring brought no change in fortune, despite the belated arrival of the updated Honda V10. It was scant consolation that this was the first race of the year in which both Lucky Strike B.A.R Hondas reached the chequered flag, albeit in ninth and 12th places. Reliability aside, the race in Germany showed that it would take a stellar effort to catch Jordan, Jaguar and the rest of their midfield rivals.

Appropriately, Silverstone proved to be the team's salvation. Lucky Strike B.A.R Honda's home track is located only seven miles away from its Brackley base and the whole factory turned up to watch Villeneuve and Panis come home fourth and fifth.

It was an odd race, this. Firstly, the conditions were unmistakably English. Dry, wet, somewhere in-between; anything and everything. The pit lane was in chaos throughout. Lucky Strike B.A.R Honda knew its fortunes lay with the rain Gods. On a wet track, not only would the power advantage of the leading teams be largely negated, but the superior Bridgestone intermediate and wet tyres would come into their own.

The track was dry for the start but, after a couple of laps, the rain started. It was light enough for the cars to stay out initially, but by lap 12 it was pouring and dry tyres had become a liability. On wets, both B.A.Rs were able to pick off their Michelin-shod opponents as predicted. With other cars sliding off, JV was elevated into the top six.

Meanwhile, David Richards had managed to get his personal helicopter airborne and his pilot flew upwind to relay crucial weather information about five minutes before it hit the track. As the rain began to abate, other teams started to switch to dry tyres, but Richards knew the coast wasn't clear and kept his drivers out for as long as possible. By the time they had to come in, sterling work by the pit crew ensured they re-emerged without losing any places. And that was the way it stayed. Villeneuve fourth, Panis fifth. Five crucial points. Smiles all round.

"It has been a long time coming but today's result is fantastic for the team," said Villeneuve afterwards. "We had two great pit stops and made the right tyre choices in very tough conditions."

EXILE ON MAIN STREET: Villeneuve in his adopted Monaco home (left) and with team boss David Richards (above). Below, Panis practises looking startled

Olivier Panis added: "I'm very happy and really pleased we were able to put on a good show for all the staff in the grandstands."

After the joy of Silverstone though, the team came back down to earth in France two weeks later with a serious reality check. Mid-grid qualifying was followed by a double DNF. F1 has always been contrary. Behind the closed doors of the team principal's motorhome, however, it was a weekend of frantic activity and David Richards penned a two-year deal with Jenson Button. The young Brit was on his way to Lucky Strike B.A.R Honda, which meant that either Villeneuve or Panis would be moving on.

Germany and Hungary were next but, unfortunately, it was the same old story – poor reliability overshadowed small improvements elsewhere. Ultimately, if you can't get your car to the finishing line, it matters not what other quantum leaps you make. At Hockenheim Panis was denied an almost certain championship point when his engine expired on lap 40, while Villeneuve's gearbox stopped him even earlier.

In Hungary, where the team had introduced a completely new front wing to meet the demands of the tight, twisting circuit, Villeneuve failed to finish while Panis battled his way to 12th place. Battled? Well, after a truly awful start the Frenchman showed real character and reeled off highly creditable lap times in pursuit of very little.

News that Olivier Panis would drive for Toyota in 2003 broke during the week leading up to the Belgian GP and came as something of a surprise. Previously it was known that Button and Villeneuve had cast–iron contracts for 2003; Olivier didn't. Three drivers don't go into two cars so Panis did the smart thing and secured his own future before it was decided for him.

AT HOCKENHEIM PANIS WAS DENIED AN ALMOST CERTAIN CHAMPIONSHIP POINT WHEN HIS ENGINE EXPIRED ON LAP 40

For the ultra-quick Spa circuit the team reverted to its old front wing. A troublesome qualifying session left the cars down in 13th (Villeneuve) and 15th (Panis) – and again both were slow off the start line.

Panis had an abject day but was put out of his misery near the end when his Honda expired, so he was classified 12th. Villeneuve settled quickly, however, and once he'd cleared some "defensive" driving by Giancarlo Fisichella, he quickly passed Allan McNish's Toyota. He kept up his pace throughout and began picking up positions as drivers in front of him blew up. Towards the end he had closed right in on Mika Salo, Irvine and the final championship point, but he ran out of laps. Nevertheless, it was an excellent drive by the determined Canadian.

Next up was the Italian GP – and the team was confident of doing well. After all, it had scored points on its last two visits to the legendary Monza track. And so it turned out. This time it was Panis who did the honours. With his GP future well and truly settled, he produced his most

convincing display of the year, gaining six positions on the opening lap and benefiting from a few retirements thereafter. He crossed the line sixth and said: "To get a point after starting 16th is fantastic. I took the risk of a two-stop strategy and it worked."

The United States GP at Indianapolis was the season's penultimate race. Villeneuve recorded his best grid position of the year and went on to score a point. Team-mate Panis, on the other hand, couldn't get away quickly enough. Weekend-long problems were compounded by another awful start and persistent mechanical difficulties. Not a 124th GP to remember for Olivier, but two points in as many races had helped the team to leap-frog Honda rival Jordan in the championship. A point more than Jaguar in Suzuka and the team would retain its place as the sixth best in F1. Game on.

So to Japan, where engine partner and track owner Honda was rumoured to be preparing a "Suzuka special" engine... although the Japanese GP was anything but the swansong Olivier Panis hoped for. In his last race for

BAR BAR RAN: Villeneuve and Panis head a midfield battle (left). Above, the team was usually very slick in the pits

Lucky Strike B.A.R Honda, he encountered early mechanical grief and pitted twice in search of a cure. At the second time of asking the Frenchman tried to rejoin, but was forced out with only eight laps done. Some *au revoir* to his Lucky Strike B.A.R Honda career but, in many ways, entirely representative of the ill luck he'd suffered during his tenure with the team. "It's always sad to be leaving," said Olivier. "This year has been tough for me but the team has made good progress and I'm glad I was able to contribute. I want to thank everyone – the race team, the test team and the people back at the factory – for all their hard work over the last two seasons. I have really enjoyed being with them. I would also like to thank Jacques for being a great team-mate. Our relationship has been very good and I wish him and the team every success for the future."

Villeneuve fared little better than his departing confrère, because an engine failure at half-distance ended his season. It was left to Jordan to snatch two points from the race, which meant that Lucky Strike B.A.R Honda finished the season eighth. It was the team's worst showing since its debut year in 1999, but, on reflection, probably not an unfair placing. Afterwards Villeneuve said: "At least we've made progress throughout this season and this is the first time that has happened at Lucky Strike B.A.R Honda, so that's a positive. Next year will definitely be a lot better so we have to look forward now,"

So while Lucky Strike B.A.R Honda might have little to celebrate from a frustrating year of upheaval and change, there are definite signs that things will be better in 2003. In fact, many seasoned F1 observers agree with Villeneuve's positive vibe. They predict that any team drawing on the financial clout of British American Tobacco, the sole attention of Honda, the technical nous of Geoffrey Willis and his talented, hugely dedicated team plus Richards' undoubted leadership ability can only go one way – and that is up.

The final word comes from the main man. David Richards has a huge challenge ahead of him as he tries to turn this team into a contender for regular points finishes and, ultimately, grand prix wins. Big as the task might seem though, you are always left with the impression that the size of this ambition never exceeds the scope of his talent.

He says: "I never underestimated the challenge of transforming Lucky Strike B.A.R Honda into a future world championship contender and the same is true of our partner Honda. We have endured some difficult times this season but have worked together to overcome our problems and make steady but significant progress. I would like to thank the team for all its hard work and congratulate the staff on a job well done. It has been a very tough season but when I look at where we started and where we are now, I am convinced that this level of commitment from everyone at Lucky Strike B.A.R Honda bodes well for some rewarding times ahead."

PETRONAS MALAYSIAN GRAND PRIX

FURNACE-LIKE HEAT, MICHELIN TYRES AND A FIRST-CORNER SCUFFLE WERE ENOUGH TO BEAT FERRARI IN MALAYSIA. BUT IT WAS STILL A SCHUEY WHO TOOK THE FLAG

GUERRILLAS IN THE MIST: Schuey and Montoya emerge from the Kuala Lumpur heat haze en route to driving into each other at the first corner. This left Ralf to win (inset) without actually having to race

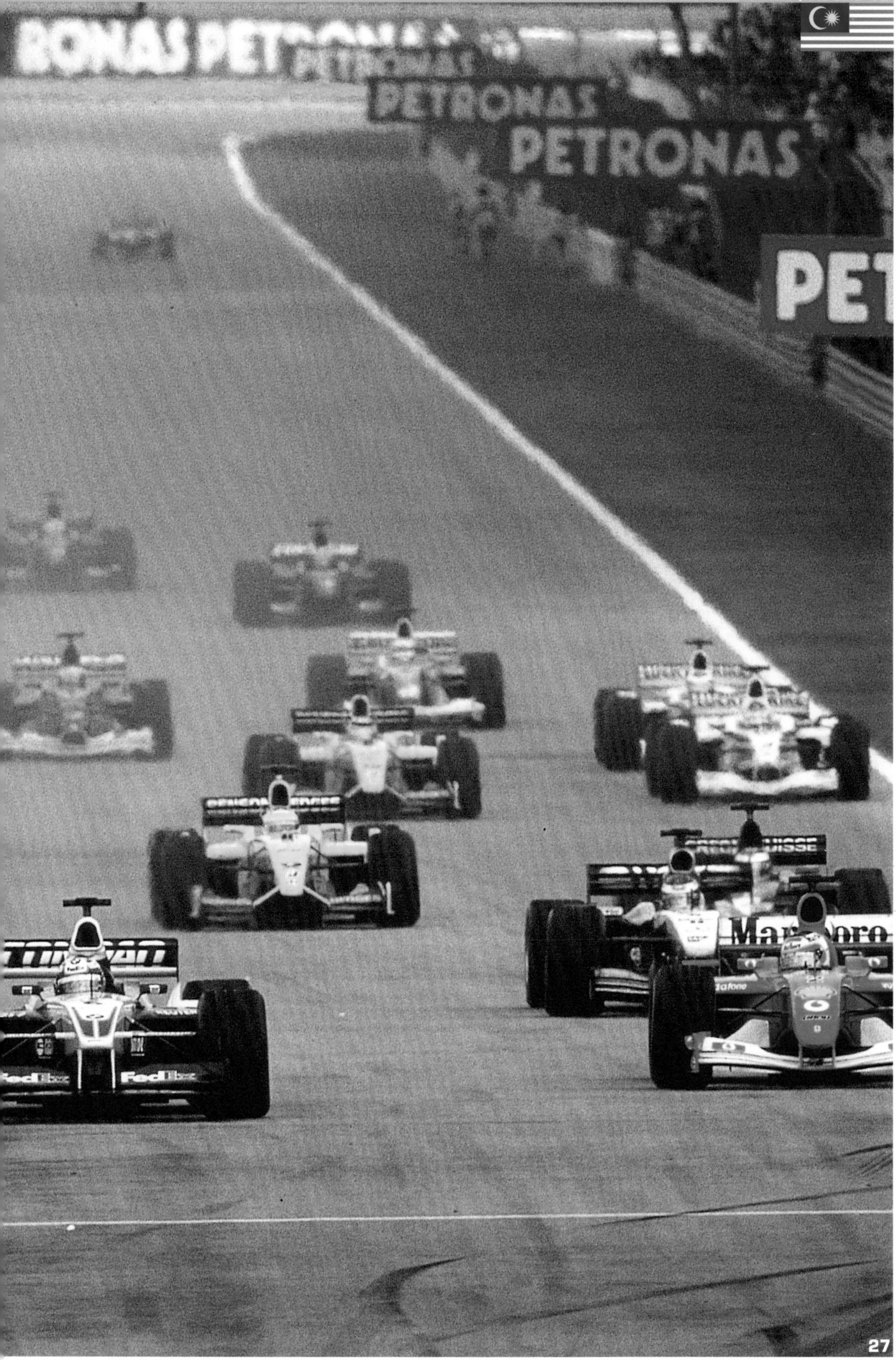
PETRONAS
PETRONAS
FedEx
FedEx

SEPANG. IT WAS THE RACE THAT GAVE THEM all false hope. If Ferrari had mopped up in Melbourne with its old car, at least Williams-BMW managed to hit back in the searing heat of Malaysia.

Yes, you could say that with track temperatures approaching 50 degrees, Williams and Michelin were in much better shape. And yes, you could point out that Ralf Schumacher used a one-stop strategy to better effect than a two-stopping Rubens Barrichello, whose challenge was ultimately scuppered by that rarest of all things, a blown Ferrari V10. But the reality was that with Michael Schumacher and Juan Pablo Montoya making contact at the first corner (see right) it was all relatively simple for Ralf. We didn't actually find out what might have been.

Michael kept his 100 per cent Malaysian pole position record firmly in place, with Montoya a quarter of a second adrift. But Sunday, Michael knew, would be altogether tougher. The Bridgestone wear rates were higher than Michelin's and there was no prospect of Ferrari doing a one-stop race, even if it wanted to.

At Williams they hedged their bets. According to chief operations engineer Sam Michael's simulations, a two-stop run was about eight seconds faster over a race distance. Providing, of course, that you could run at your own pace. But with Michael on the pole, what were the chances of getting by?

Montoya went the two-stop route, which explained, perhaps, his heavy-handedness at the first corner. Ralf, meanwhile, went for one. "I've only once made a two-stop run work for me," he pointed out.

But with the king and his pretender tangling at the first turn and Rubens failing to last the distance, it was a walk in the park for Ralf. He let Rubens open up a small lead at first and then stabilised the gap. So easily, in fact, that you suspected they were on the same strategy and that Ralf had merely been looking after the rubber early on. But when Rubens pitted at one-third distance and Ralf sailed serenely on, you knew Williams had it in the bag.

The question is: would a two-stopping Schuey or Juan Pablo have beaten Ralf? We will never know. "I think it would have been very close," Sam Michael said.

Ralf's only other concern was his tyres. This had nothing to do with their performance or grip after 30-lap stints of Sepang but was more about their look. Mindful that nothing

WITH THE KING AND HIS PRETENDER TANGLING AT THE FIRST TURN AND RUBENS FAILING TO LAST THE DISTANCE, IT WAS A WALK IN THE PARK FOR RALF

THE CAR IN FRONT REALLY IS A TOYOTA: Villeneuve chases Trulli (below). Note that Sepang gets rave reviews for its facilities, even though the grandstand roof appears to be an old astraglide. Above, from left: crap move by Sato on Fisichella; irresistible force and immovable object

JUAN HIT BLUNDER

ALL THINGS considered, it was a bit of a travesty. There was Juan Pablo Montoya, using his BMW grunt to challenge Michael Schumacher's pole position Ferrari at the first corner. Contact was made. Michael needed to stop for a new nose and Juan Pablo rejoined near the back. A racing incident, surely? No, said the stewards, who handed the Colombian a drive-through penalty.

A what? This was not some dubious belly-filler to be grabbed when you and the kids are late back, but a new-for-2002 slap on the wrist that is not quite as bad as a stop-and-go. You don't actually have to stop, but just crawl down the pit lane at the kind of speed that makes you think you have.

Montoya (above) was not amused. "We were racing," he pointed out, "which, I thought, was what we were supposed to be doing. If people don't want to see that kind of stuff maybe we should get the Safety Car out and run behind it all afternoon."

It was a good point, well made. People like to see that kind of stuff. And, in the circumstances, they were always going to.

Montoya wasn't dangerous, just a little naïve perhaps.

Off the line Schuey had performed his usual chop and Montoya carried a little more momentum down to Turn One. The Williams had its nose in front but not significantly. A quarter of a car's length, maybe, but not enough to turn in on the Ferrari.

Montoya's plan was to squeeze Michael, run side-by-side with him through the first corner and have the inside for Turn Two. But he squeezed a little too hard, Michael ran onto the kerb and the Ferrari slid wide into the Williams, losing its nose and pushing Juan Pablo onto the marbles.

Montoya was always going to muscle Michael – and the world champion was never going to back down. Sometimes you need an incident, just to establish boundaries. If Schumacher ceded his ground Montoya would log it in the mental file and pull the stunt on a fortnightly basis. It was the very definition of a racing incident.

BIKINI ATOLL: two passers-by get in the way and mar an otherwise perfectly good shot of a BAR truck

BOTH McLARENS SUCCUMBED TO ENGINE FAILURE AND WITH TWO RACES DOWN THE TEAM DIDN'T HAVE A POINT ON THE BOARD

would turn off the fans quicker than protests over tyres and races decided in law courts weeks later, the FIA always said that it would apply discretion to what did or did not constitute a grooved tyre. Wearing out the grooves was okay: what the governing body did not want to see was tyres that quickly wore down to near-slick state and performed better in that condition.

Despite the shot state of Ralf's rubber, especially the outer grooves, he set his fastest race time immediately prior to his 'in' lap. You wondered about a protest from a Bridgestone team – read Ferrari – but it didn't come. And FIA technical director Charlie Whiting was happy that Ralf's time was nothing more than a driver pushing hard on a light fuel load with tyres that had no performance drop-off.

Montoya recovered to finish second but nobody else was remotely in it, which was something of a blow to David Coulthard. With Mika Häkkinen changing nappies and lying on a beach, this was supposed to be DC's big title year.

"My goal was to challenge for race wins and the championship," he lamented, "but now it looks as if I might have to refocus my sights on scoring points. Which is very frustrating." Both McLarens succumbed to engine failure and with two races down the team didn't have a point on the board.

Re-establishing himself well at Renault, Jenson Button was on course for a podium finish until a rear suspension problem made him easy prey for Schuey's recovering Ferrari. The Saubers claimed the remaining points with Nick Heidfeld fifth and Brazilian rookie Felipe Massa scoring in just his second race for the team.

For BMW, it was a first one-two, something it never achieved back in the Brabham-BMW days. The bad news? Ferrari's F2002 was just around the corner.

FLASHBACK
October 17 1999. Sepang, Malaysia

THIS IS WHERE THE CONCEPT OF A RETRO sidebar falls short, because prior to 2002 there had only been three world championship grands prix in Malaysia. Still, the first was more than averagely memorable.

Michael Schumacher was racing for the first time since breaking a leg at Silverstone the previous July. Rivals wondered whether the injury might have dulled his edge: he answered by beating team-mate Eddie Irvine to pole by 0.947 seconds. Any more questions?

In Michael's absence Irvine had hauled himself into world title contention and was two points shy of McLaren star Mika Häkkinen with a couple of races remaining. Schuey was here to help.

He could not have done more. He waved Irvine through and then proceeded to fluctuate his pace to frustrate the following Häkkinen (above), who was completely flaked out by the end. "It was the hardest race of my life," he said. "Michael was lifting off in high-speed corners and I had to be careful not to run into him." He conceded, however, that Ferrari had, tactically, been "brilliant".

Two hours after the race, the bombshell: the Ferraris, undertrays were not quite the right shape and the cars were excluded. Häkkinen was champion for the second time in as many years, but a few days later an FIA court of appeal overturned that decision. The Ferraris were reinstated, Irvine led the points chase and everything was set up for a title shoot-out in Japan, which the Ulsterman lost.

But for a few days Eddie was on top of the world. "Not only is Michael the best number one in the business," he said, "but he's the best number two as well."

BRITAIN'S BEST-SELLING SINGLES... WEREN'T EXACTLY OF T-REX QUALITY WHEN SCHUEY BAMBOOZLED MIKA

1 EIFFEL 65	Blue (Da Ba De)
2 SHANIA TWAIN	Man! I Feel Like A Woman
3 CHRISTINE AGUILERA	Genie In A Bottle
4 S CLUB 7	S Club Party
5 BRITNEY SPEARS	You Drive Me Craz

March 17 2002
SEPANG CIRCUIT
KUALA LUMPUR
CIRCUIT LENGTH: 3.444miles / 5.543km

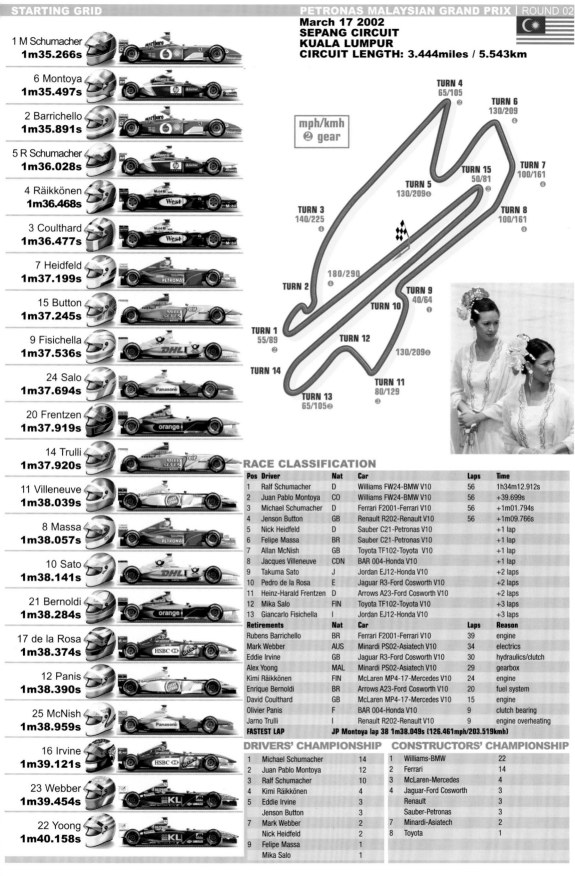

1 M Schumacher
1m35.266s

6 Montoya
1m35.497s

2 Barrichello
1m35.891s

5 R Schumacher
1m36.028s

4 Räikkönen
1m36.468s

3 Coulthard
1m36.477s

7 Heidfeld
1m37.199s

15 Button
1m37.245s

9 Fisichella
1m37.536s

24 Salo
1m37.694s

20 Frentzen
1m37.919s

14 Trulli
1m37.920s

11 Villeneuve
1m38.039s

8 Massa
1m38.057s

10 Sato
1m38.141s

21 Bernoldi
1m38.284s

17 de la Rosa
1m38.374s

12 Panis
1m38.390s

25 McNish
1m38.959s

16 Irvine
1m39.121s

23 Webber
1m39.454s

22 Yoong
1m40.158s

mph/kmh
② gear

TURN 4 65/105 ②
TURN 6 130/209 ④
TURN 5 130/209 ①
TURN 15 50/81 ②
TURN 7 100/161 ④
TURN 3 140/225 ①
TURN 8 100/161 ④
180/290 ①
TURN 2 ①
TURN 9 40/64 ①
TURN 10
TURN 1 55/89 ②
TURN 12
130/209 ①
TURN 14
TURN 11 80/129 ③
TURN 13 65/105 ②

RACE CLASSIFICATION

Pos	Driver	Nat	Car	Laps	Time
1	Ralf Schumacher	D	Williams FW24-BMW V10	56	1h34m12.912s
2	Juan Pablo Montoya	CO	Williams FW24-BMW V10	56	+39.699s
3	Michael Schumacher	D	Ferrari F2001-Ferrari V10	56	+1m01.794s
4	Jenson Button	GB	Renault R202-Renault V10	56	+1m09.766s
5	Nick Heidfeld	D	Sauber C21-Petronas V10		+1 lap
6	Felipe Massa	BR	Sauber C21-Petronas V10		+1 lap
7	Allan McNish	GB	Toyota TF102-Toyota V10		+1 lap
8	Jacques Villeneuve	CDN	BAR 004-Honda V10		+1 lap
9	Takuma Sato	J	Jordan EJ12-Honda V10		+2 laps
10	Pedro de la Rosa	E	Jaguar R3-Ford Cosworth V10		+2 laps
11	Heinz-Harald Frentzen	D	Arrows A23-Ford Cosworth V10		+2 laps
12	Mika Salo	FIN	Toyota TF102-Toyota V10		+3 laps
13	Giancarlo Fisichella	I	Jordan EJ12-Honda V10		+3 laps

Retirements	Nat	Car	Laps	Reason
Rubens Barrichello	BR	Ferrari F2001-Ferrari V10	39	engine
Mark Webber	AUS	Minardi PS02-Asiatech V10	34	electrics
Eddie Irvine	GB	Jaguar R3-Ford Cosworth V10	30	hydraulics/clutch
Alex Yoong	MAL	Minardi PS02-Asiatech V10	29	gearbox
Kimi Räikkönen	FIN	McLaren MP4-17-Mercedes V10	24	engine
Enrique Bernoldi	BR	Arrows A23-Ford Cosworth V10	20	fuel system
David Coulthard	GB	McLaren MP4-17-Mercedes V10	15	engine
Olivier Panis	F	BAR 004-Honda V10	9	clutch bearing
Jarno Trulli	I	Renault R202-Renault V10	9	engine overheating

FASTEST LAP JP Montoya lap 38 1m38.049s (126.461mph/203.519kmh)

DRIVERS' CHAMPIONSHIP

1	Michael Schumacher	14
2	Juan Pablo Montoya	12
3	Ralf Schumacher	10
4	Kimi Räikkönen	4
5	Eddie Irvine	3
	Jenson Button	3
7	Mark Webber	2
	Nick Heidfeld	2
9	Felipe Massa	1
	Mika Salo	1

CONSTRUCTORS' CHAMPIONSHIP

1	Williams-BMW	22
2	Ferrari	14
3	McLaren-Mercedes	4
4	Jaguar-Ford Cosworth	3
	Renault	3
	Sauber-Petronas	3
	Minardi-Asiatech	2
8	Toyota	1

Marlboro

FLESH CORDON

THE MOST CONSISTENT FACTORS DURING THE 2002
F1 SEASON? FERRARI'S RACE PERFORMANCE, THE
SECOND MINARDI'S GRID POSITION AND THE ABILITY
OF SOME PEOPLE TO ACCESS ALL AREAS DESPITE
NOT WEARING A PASS. OR, INDEED, MUCH ELSE

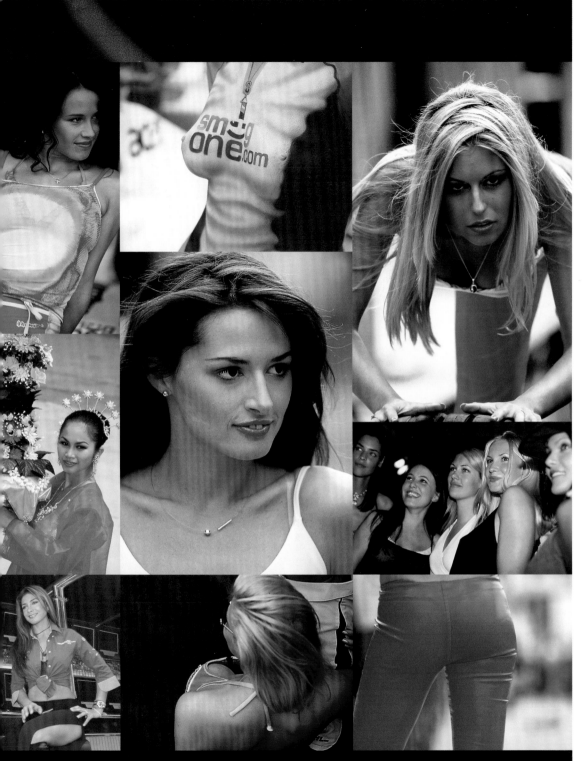

GIRL TORQUE: a few of last summer's migrant paddock visitors. Excuse me, girl in the middle and you in the top left-hand corner, would you mind looking at the camera, please?

GRANDE PREMIO DO BRASIL

LESSON NUMBER ONE:
DO NOT COLLIDE WITH
MICHAEL SCHUMACHER
ON THE OPENING LAP.
AT LEAST, TRY NOT TO
DO IT EVERY BLOODY
WEEKEND..

SCARLET O'HARDER: note that one of the cars below has a front wing, the other doesn't. There is a reason for this. Miffed after being biffed by Schuey, Montoya sought solace from fiancée Connie (above)

THIS SHOULD HAVE BEEN JUAN PABLO MONTOYA'S DAY.
Should.

It was in Brazil one year earlier that the Colombian had outlined his credentials for heroism within the Formula One parish by bullying Michael Schumacher into submission and controlling the race until a snoozing – and lapped – Jos Verstappen bulldozed him off the track.

That performance certainly made its mark with the locals. Interlagos spectators are fiercely pro-Rubens Barrichello by tradition, but before the race they were asked to vote for their favourite driver... and nominated Montoya ahead of their fellow Paulista. That probably didn't hurt Rubens quite as much, however, as the new nickname fans had coined for him: the artist formerly known as Rubinho was now Burrinho – little donkey, in Portuguese.

Sensing potential trouble from Williams post-Malaysia, Ferrari chose to wheel out its latest F2002 chassis for the first time at a race. At least, it brought along one of them. No prizes for guessing who had first call, but Michael Schumacher's shiny new toy was not enough to deprive the on-fire Montoya of his fourth F1 career pole. But then Montoya fluffed his start and allowed Schuey, casually, to muscle him aside at the first corner.

Juan Pablo promptly proved that he can be every bit as impatient as he is fast by trying to draft alongside his rival on the approach to Turn Three. Incorrect. Michael was within his rights to pull across: cue lots of shattered blue and white carbon fibre. "I didn't feel anything, to be honest," Michael said later. He might have noticed, however, that there was no longer anything in his mirrors apart from clouds of tyre smoke as 20 cars attempted to avoid Montoya's disintegrating wing.

THE CROWD COULD BE HEARD CHANTING FOR THE FIRST TIME ALL WEEKEND WHEN BARRICHELLO RASPED INTO SECOND PLACE

THE LEAST WE CAN DO IS WAVE TO EACH OTHER: Rubens forgets to untape his earpiece before soaking up the plaudits (above); Coulthard tracks down Button (left)

The remains were spread liberally down the straight, leaving Giancarlo Fisichella and Allan McNish little option but to run into them. Both pitted for repairs along with the wing's owner, who managed to scramble back to fifth place by flagfall.

And that was it as far as challenges to Michael were concerned. Barrichello lined up only eighth: true, he had been deprived of his quickest lap time for jumping a red light in the pit lane on Saturday, but he would still have started in the same place because his best two laps were a) very similar and b) both crap.

Ferrari put him on a double-stop strategy in an effort to gain track position – and it was obvious from the way he sliced through the field that everybody else at the head of the pack intended to pit only once.

Obvious to anybody who didn't have a Brazilian passport, that is... The crowd was mildly delirious about its former favourite's initial burst of speed and could actually be heard chanting for the first time all weekend when he rasped into second place and set after Schuey, who obligingly stepped aside to allow Rubens to gain maximum effect from his sprint-race trim. Team calculations suggested Barrichello would probably have finished third after two stops, but shortly after taking

MEDICAL SCAR

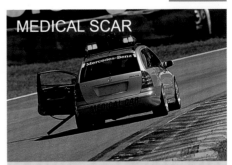

SUNDAY MORNING'S PRE-RACE WARM-UP IS usually a fairly tame affair. Its main purpose is to give drivers 30 minutes to check the balance of their chassis, but for fans who skip qualifying it offers a first chance to see their heroes in action.

In the blistering heat it was also the only thing they had to watch apart from the grand prix, because the sole supporting race – the opening round of the FIA Formula 3000 series – took place on Saturday.

That was not, however, why Enrique Bernoldi chose to spice things up. The Arrows driver just lost control, pure and simple, as he sped through the Senna S and his car slammed into the wall backwards at the bottom of the hill. The Arrows was completely trashed and ruptured oil lines led to a brief, spectacular flash fire.

With the accident happening so close to the pit lane exit, the FIA's official Mercedes-Benz Medical Car was on the scene within moments. As, indeed, were Michael Schumacher's Ferrari and Nick Heidfeld's Sauber. Schuey picked his way through the debris and steered to the right of the wreck while Heidfeld, unsighted, went to the left – which was just where former F1 racer Alex Ribeiro had parked the Medical Car. And he was just about to get out.

Fortunately he spotted that the grass verge contained a fast-approaching Sauber and stayed where he was. Heidfeld careened into the swinging Merc door and came to rest against the barriers. The consequences for both could have been awful.

Heidfeld enjoys a post-season glass of beer (singular), but that's usually about as wild as he gets. "I didn't see any yellow warning flags," he said, slightly shaken.

The stewards hauled him away for a chat and, after reviewing video evidence, concluded that the flag marshals had been too busy watching Bernoldi's shunt to remember what they were supposed to be there for. Heidfeld was cleared of any wrongdoing and might have scored a point in the race but for a weird, brake-related vibration that led to his retirement.

NOT NOW, CATERER: former sandwich delivery boy Massa fends off Villeneuve and Frentzen (above); brotherly hugs (left); a Brazilian, yesterday (below)

THE WILLIAMS APPEARED TO HAVE A CLEAR PERFORMANCE EDGE BUT SCHUEY JNR DIDN'T SEEM VERY KEEN ON USING IT

the lead he had to make an unscheduled one by the side of the track because the F2001's hydraulics packed up.

Michael, who hadn't retired from a race since July 29 the previous year, ambled on. His younger brother Ralf later gave chase, but although the Williams appeared to have a clear performance edge Schuey Jnr didn't seem very keen on using it. For lap after lap he towed up behind Michael going into the first turn, but not once did he muster a whiff of a challenge. Would Montoya have been so submissive in that situation? Not a chance; more's the pity he had already screwed up by then.

The traction-efficient Renaults beat the McLarens off the line, but although David Coulthard repassed Jenson Button fairly swiftly he had to wait until his refuelling stop to edge past Jarno Trulli. Good pitwork also helped Kimi Räikkönen get ahead of the Anglo-French cars, but the Finn retired with hub failure four laps from the end. Engine failure had put paid to Trulli half a dozen laps earlier, so Button came through to take fourth from the recovering Montoya and Mika Salo, whose Corollaesque reliability earned Toyota its second point in only three starts.

There was disappointment, however, for Felipe Massa, who lined up 12th for his maiden home GP but crashed out after 43 laps. Still, that was progress: a couple of years earlier the Sauber driver had worked in the paddock as a sandwich delivery boy.

FLASHBACK
January 26, 1975. Interlagos, Brazil

HAS THERE EVER BEEN A MORE ELEGANT Formula One combination?

Firstly there was the Brabham BT44B, a classic Gordon Murray design and one of the most outstanding examples of Seventies racing architecture. Stylish. Balanced. Fast.

And at the wheel was Carlos Pace (above), with his simple, striking crash helmet design: black with two yellow arrows, its looks alone were probably worth two-tenths per lap.

Pace joined Brabham in 1974 after walking out on Team Surtees and the partnership swiftly gelled.

The 1975 campaign started promisingly when he qualified on the front row in Argentina, but his engine blew while he lay second. Two weeks later he was only sixth on the grid for his home race, but he surged into third place at the start and picked off team-mate Carlos Reutemann on lap 14. By then, however, Jean-Pierre Jarier's Shadow DN5 was already more than 20 seconds up the road. Pace's car was working well, but not that well...

Then, on lap 33 of 40, Jarier stopped with a failed fuel metering unit. Pace was gifted the lead and São Paulo erupted. But it was to be his only win.

Poor reliability plagued him during the rest of that season and he spent the following year helping to develop a new Alfa Romeo flat-12. It was sorted by 1977, when he finished second in the opening Argentine GP, but shortly after the third race in South Africa a friend persuaded Pace to join him for a private plane trip. In bad weather they hit a mountain and that distinctive black-and-yellow helmet would never be seen again.

BRITAIN'S BEST-SELLING SINGLES... WHEN LUCK WAS ON CARLOS PACE'S SIDE FOR ONCE	
1 RALPH McTELL	Streets of London
2 STATUS QUO	Down Down
3 MUD	Lonely This Christmas
4 KENNY	The Bump
5 GLORIA GAYNOR	Never Can Say Goodbye

March 31 2002
AUTODROMO JOSÉ CARLOS PACE
INTERLAGOS
SÃO PAULO
CIRCUIT LENGTH: 2.677miles / 4.309km

Starting Grid

Pos	Driver	Time
	6 Montoya	1m13.114s
	1 M Schumacher	1m13.241s
	5 R Schumacher	1m13.328s
	3 Coulthard	1m13.565s
	4 Räikkönen	1m13.595s
	14 Trulli	1m13.611s
	15 Button	1m13.665s
	2 Barrichello	1m13.935s
	7 Heidfeld	1m14.223s
	24 Salo	1m 14.443s
	17 de la Rosa	1m14.464s
	8 Massa	1m14.533s
	16 Irvine	1m14.537s
	9 Fisichella	1m14.748s
	11 Villeneuve	1m14.760s
	25 McNish	1m14.990s
	12 Panis	1m14.996s
	20 Frentzen	1m15.112s
	10 Sato	1m15.296s
	23 Webber	1m15.340s
	21 Bernoldi	1m15.355s
	22 Yoong	1m16.728s

mph/kmh
❷ gear

CURVA DO SOL 130/209 ❹
DESCIDA DO SOL 85/138 ❷
RETA OPOSTA
'S' DO SENNA 55/89 ❷
SUBIDA DO LAGO 78/125 ❸
FERRA DURA
PINEIRINHO 60/97 ❷
MERGULHO 118/190 ❸
LARANJA
JUNCAO
ARQUEBAN CADA
BICO DE PATO 45/72 ❶
SUBIDA DOS BOXES 160/258 ❻

RACE CLASSIFICATION

Pos	Driver	Nat	Car	Laps	Time
1	Michael Schumacher	D	Ferrari F2002-Ferrari V10	71	1h31m43.663s
2	Ralf Schumacher	D	Williams FW24-BMW V10	71	+0.588s
3	David Coulthard	GB	McLaren MP4-17-Mercedes V10	71	+59.110s
4	Jenson Button	GB	Renault R202-Renault V10	71	+1m06.883s
5	Juan Pablo Montoya	CO	Williams FW24-BMW V10	71	+1m07.563s
6	Mika Salo	FIN	Toyota TF102-Toyota V10		+1 lap
7	Eddie Irvine	GB	Jaguar R3-Ford Cosworth V10		+1 lap
8	Pedro de la Rosa	E	Jaguar R3-Ford Cosworth V10		+1 lap
9	Takuma Sato	J	Jordan EJ12-Honda V10		+2 laps
10	Jacques Villeneuve	CDN	BAR 004-Honda V10		+3 laps
11	Mark Webber	AUS	Minardi PS02-Asiatech V10		+3 laps
12	Kimi Räikkönen	FIN	McLaren MP4-17-Mercedes V10		+4 laps
13	Alex Yoong	MAL	Minardi PS02-Asiatech V10		+4 laps

Retirements	Nat	Car	Laps	Reason
Nick Heidfeld	D	Sauber C21-Petronas V10	61	brake disc
Jarno Trulli	I	Renault R202-Renault V10	60	engine
Felipe Massa	BR	Sauber C21-Petronas V10	41	accident
Allan McNish	GB	Toyota TF102-Toyota V10	40	wheel bearing/spin
Olivier Panis	F	BAR 004-Honda V10	25	gearbox
Heinz-Harald Frentzen	D	Arrows A23-Ford Cosworth V10	25	suspension
Enrique Bernoldi	BR	Arrows A23-Ford Cosworth V10	19	suspension
Rubens Barrichello	BR	Ferrari F2001-Ferrari V10	16	hydraulics
Giancarlo Fisichella	I	Jordan EJ12-Honda V10	6	engine

FASTEST LAP JP Montoya lap 60 1m16.079s (126.697mph/203.899kmh)

DRIVERS' CHAMPIONSHIP

1	Michael Schumacher	24
2	Ralf Schumacher	16
3	Juan Pablo Montoya	14
4	Jenson Button	6
5	Kimi Räikkönen	4
	David Coulthard	4
7	Eddie Irvine	3
8	Mark Webber	2
	Nick Heidfeld	2
	Mika Salo	2
11	Felipe Massa	1

CONSTRUCTORS' CHAMPIONSHIP

1	Williams-BMW	30
2	Ferrari	24
3	McLaren-Mercedes	8
4	Renault	6
5	Jaguar-Ford Cosworth	3
	Sauber-Petronas	3
7	Minardi-Asiatech	2
	Toyota	2

WHEN ALLAN McNISH LINED UP ON THE GRID for the opening grand prix of 2002 in Melbourne it marked the end of a long, arduous and frequently unjust journey for a driver who ought to have been given a chance among the sport's elite many years before.

The Scot originally exploded into the junior motor racing mainstream in 1987, when as a relatively unknown karting graduate he began shaking up the leading lights in Britain's senior Formula Ford championship.

At the end of that year he took part in a Marlboro evaluation test and was selected to drive alongside Mika Häkkinen in the tobacco giant's new-for-1988 Formula Vauxhall Lotus team. There wasn't much to choose between them and they collected one championship title apiece – McNish the British, Häkkinen the European.

Within a couple of seasons McNish's career had accelerated ahead of the Finn's. He was racing in the FIA F3000 series and had a three-year F1 testing deal with McLaren... but after 1991 his sponsor dropped him for the sake of one bad season. Move ahead 10 years and McNish had still to start an F1 race while Häkkinen had retired from the sport with 20 GP wins and two world titles under his belt.

At the time of writing it looks as though McNish's F1 career will be restricted to a single season. A couple of days before the Belgian GP Toyota announced it would be dropping both its drivers. This was rough justice for McNish, who had spent much of the past couple of seasons developing the team's fledgling grand prix car. In 2002 he didn't quite match team-mate Mika Salo in qualifying, but in terms of race speed they were very even and only bad luck prevented him scoring top-six finishes in Malaysia and Italy. With a year of experience under his belt he would have been ideally placed to take a big step forward with the team in 2003, but it's not to be. It would have been an even greater injustice, however, had his name never appeared on a grand prix grid at all.

"Things have been a little bit frustrating in terms of overall results," he says. "I lost one point in Malaysia and a possible three in Monza – and those would have put me 12th in the championship, which I think would have been respectable. It would certainly have put a completely different slant on my season. It's a small consolation that I didn't drop out of either of those races through any fault of my own."

Prior to his extraordinarily violent accident during qualifying in Japan (a 57g rear impact complete with backward somersault and triple pike that left him a) on the wrong side of the barriers and b) nursing only a bruised knee, see page 139), the most significant blip of his campaign came in Monaco, where he clipped a barrier while running strongly and trying to force his way past Salo.

"That apart," he says, "most of the problems have been technical and beyond my control. Overall, knowing what I know, I am satisfied with the way I have performed, although with the benefit of hindsight I might have done a few things slightly differently. At the start of the season for instance, the engineers and I were forever changing

THE LONG AND GRINDING ROAD

ALLAN McNISH WAS THE JENSON BUTTON OF A PREVIOUS GENERATION, A 20-YEAR-OLD WHO HAD THE WORLD AT ITS FEET. TROUBLE WAS, THE WORLD MOVED UNEXPECTEDLY AND ANY CHANCE OF AN F1 CAREER BEGAN TO LOOK INCREASINGLY REMOTE. THEN TOYOTA BEGAN CASTING AROUND FOR THE SCOT'S TELEPHONE NUMBER..

TOYOTA STORY: tipped as a likely F1 candidate in the early Nineties, McNish's career hit rock bottom before he bounced back to earn an F1 break about 10 years behind schedule

NORTH CAREER – A SCOTSMAN THROUGH THE AGES: success in the ALMS (top) – cheer up, Allan, there'll be an Audi R8 along in a moment. Above, from left: with *GPY*'s editor at Le Mans in 1999; rather more usefully, collecting an Autosport Award from Ron Dennis 10 years earlier; the spoils of F3 success. Below, from left: an F3000 rookie at Pau in 1990; a seasoned veteran heading for Le Mans glory in 1998

little details when we really didn't need to, but that was a product of inexperience and I learned from it. By the end of the year I was a lot better at getting more out of the car, irrespective of whether or not the chassis suited the track."

Toyota spent 2001 preparing intently for its F1 debut – and this incorporated a dummy grand prix in Austria, where the team simulated every last element of a race weekend – including having its drivers sit in an empty media room for 30 minutes, to answer non-existent questions from absent journalists. Such attention to detail couldn't fully prepare McNish for what lay in store, however.

"We might have spent a year testing," he says, "but when it boils down to it that's no preparation for a year of racing. We have learned more during this season than we did just pounding round on our own in 2001. It is disappointing that I won't get the chance to build on everything I have learned with Toyota, because with a year of racing under my belt I would be fully prepared. In Australia, for instance, I would know exactly what was needed to get the most from the weekend."

"I AM NOW AN F1 DRIVER LOOKING FOR A JOB. THAT'S A MUCH BETTER SITUATION THAN MANY IN WHICH I FOUND MYSELF EARLIER IN MY CAREER"

A number of things took him by surprise during his maiden F1 campaign. "It has been easier to race than I imagined it would be," he says. "Overtaking is difficult, but not impossible. The hardest part has been learning how to anticipate the way a track evolves during the weekend. It is probably quite a simple process for Ferrari, but when you and the team are new to F1 it becomes a bit trickier. Sometimes there has been a sudden shift in our pace and we weren't always sure why."

Some elements he found distasteful, too. He says: "Even before I had started my first race in Australia people were coming up and saying, 'I hear they are going to replace you after the first three races. How do you feel?' I couldn't believe I was hearing that kind of thing so soon. I was gobsmacked. It seemed totally stupid."

Generally, however, the season brought more positives than negatives. "After such a long wait for an F1 race opportunity I have a certain sense of fulfilment that I finally got my chance," he says, "although if I hadn't ever made it I wouldn't have lost any sleep. It has been a hard year but I enjoyed it. It was nice during free practice in Monaco on Thursday, for instance, when I came through Ste Devote and saw 'A McNish – P1' on the giant video screen. You remember moments like that.

"I accept that I might have to bow out of F1 and look at other opportunities, but I don't see any point moping. Besides, I am now an F1 driver looking for a job. That's a much better situation than many in which I found myself earlier in my career."

GETTING TO F1 THE ALLAN McNISH WAY

1980-1986	Karting, lots of success in Scotland and the rest of Britain
1987	Formula Ford (above), mostly at junior level but memorably beat all the seniors in one race at Snetterton; snapped up as official Marlboro driver after end-of-season evaluation test
1988	Formula Vauxhall Lotus, Dragon Racing – British champion
1989	British F3, WSR, second overall
1990	FIA F3000, DAMS, two wins, fourth overall; F1 test driver for McLaren
1991	FIA F3000, DAMS, one fifth place (car was crap); McLaren F1 testing; dropped from Marlboro's main driver roster at the end of the year
1992	FIA F3000 part season, 3001 International, one third place; some McLaren F1 testing
1993	Racing not pictured; tested F1 Benetton

1994	One FIA F3000 start for Vortex Motorsport in Pau, standing in for Williams-bound David Coulthard
1995	FIA F3000, PSR, two poles, seventh overall
1996	Bit of Benetton F1 testing
1997	GT racing, Porsche, three wins in North America
1998	FIA GT Championship, Porsche, fifth overall; better news – he shared the winning Porsche GT1 at Le Mans
1999	Works Porsche deal – but team didn't race; drove for Toyota at Le Mans
2000	American Le Mans Series, Audi (above), champion; second at Le Mans
2001	Toyota F1 testing
2002	F1 – and not before time

GRAN PREMIO DI SAN MARINO

FERRARI'S F2002 MIGHT HAVE
MADE A WINNING START IN
BRAZIL, BUT WHEN FORMULA
ONE RETURNED TO EUROPE
WE SAW A GLIMPSE OF
THE NEW CAR'S CAPACITY
TO OBLITERATE

Schuey fulfils his obligation to the tifosi (main shot) after
leaving everyone bar his team-mate behind at such a rate that they might as well
have been driving Triumph Heralds. Right, the prancing hoarse

YES, THE FERRARI F2002 HAD TRIUMPHED FIRST TIME OUT at Interlagos, a track where the Scuderia has struggled a bit in recent years. The team's technical director Ross Brawn called it an "away win" – a little against the run of play. But without a spot of tactical naivety on Juan Pablo Montoya's part and a paucity of aggression from Ralf Schumacher, perhaps, Williams-BMW might have done it.

Imola, though, was altogether different. This time it wasn't just Michael Schumacher. Rubens Barrichello joined in too and Ferrari scored its first one-two of the season.

Ralf made it onto the podium again but Williams was never in the race and his body language spoke volumes. "It's never good when somebody wins like that and there's only a fortnight to the next race," he said.

After narrowly pipping Rubens to the pole, Michael was away and gone through Turn One while his team-mate had to contend with Williams-BMW. Ralf got inside him, survived a brief lock-up into the first chicane and emerged second.

Michael disappeared as if on a different strategy, Ralf couldn't stay with him and Rubens was trapped behind the Williams. The usually feisty Montoya was 16 seconds behind the leading Ferrari after 10 laps and eight behind his own team-mate. A one-stopper, surely? Wrong. The Colombian had made a couple of set-up tweaks after the warm-up and had no balance. He wasn't a serious factor all afternoon.

And what of McLaren? It was hard to believe that David Coulthard was the pole position man at Imola 12 months earlier. Kimi Räikkönen outqualified him this time and the pair got through the first corner fifth and sixth.

Kimi was unable to hassle the struggling Montoya but managed to put a bit of breathing space between himself and DC over the first dozen laps. All you need to know about the McLaren-Mercedes performance level is that Coulthard was lapped before the end, right in front of Mercedes big cheese Jürgen Hubbert.

Anyone driving a two-stop race was due to pit at about the 20-lap mark. So when Michael ran at unabated pace until half-distance, you

BLUE SCREEN Montoya busy not being a factor (main shot); clockwise from above, bloke second from right ruins picture; tuning Button; Villeneuve finished just outside the points

HEIDFELD HAD TO STOP AGAIN THREE LAPS LATER AND, IN HIS HASTE, SPED DOWN THE PIT LANE. A DRIVE-THROUGH PENALTY FOLLOWED. FOUR PIT VISITS IN ONE AFTERNOON. NOT IN THE IDEAL STRATEGY MANUAL, THAT

knew two things. First, his Bridgestones were fast and consistent. Second, everyone else was in serious trouble.

One man with a Ferrari engine who visited the pits considerably more often was Nick Heidfeld. The German stopped on lap 19, two after Sauber team-mate Felipe Massa, but the crew was not expecting him. "I thought they'd called me in on the radio but it turns out they hadn't," Heidfeld explained. Amid the confusion they had to use Massa's refuelling rig and there was a bout of finger trouble. No juice went in. Heidfeld had to stop again three laps later and, in his haste, sped down the pit lane. A drive-through penalty followed. Four pit visits in one afternoon. Not in the ideal strategy manual, that.

Without a hot afternoon to help Michelin's tyres mask some of the Jaguar R3's problems, the Ford-owned team performed atrociously at Imola and Pedro de la Rosa propped up the grid. Schumacher lapped him at one-third distance and by the time Ralf and Rubens came across

ON THE SURFACE, IMOLA WAS ALL ABOUT Michael: pole position, a record number of grand prix starts for Ferrari (97), the first man to win four times at Imola, an extension of his record victory haul to 56. But the truth was that Rubens (above) was almost a match for him. The Brazilian had his best weekend as a Ferrari driver and could have won on merit.

On Saturday morning there was concern about the engine in Barrichello's race car so he took Michael's spare for qualifying. This was the chassis he had first run at Barcelona, when he'd been quicker than Schumacher, and he liked it a lot. On his second qualifying run, midway through the session, he shaved more than half a second from Ralf's provisional pole. Michael, by this stage, was still slower than his brother.

Ultimately Schumacher found the time and pipped Rubens by six hundredths. But he needed all four runs to do it. Barrichello had just three, the last one spoiled when someone threw dirt onto the road.

For the race Michael decided he wanted Rubens's chassis, with Michael's original race car becoming the Ferrari spare. Schumacher was cruising admittedly, but when Rubens came out of the pits after his first stop he was 16.5s behind Michael, a margin he managed to trim by three seconds before they next refuelled. He immediately lost the time again when there was a problem with the left-rear wheel nut in the pits. On lap 54, eight from the end, the message went out to back off and look after the engine. But from the first stop until then, discounting in/out laps, Rubens was quicker on 14 laps to Michael's four. And how often does anyone run quicker than Michael on Sunday afternoon?

PADDOCK SPACE, THE FINAL FRONTIER: McLaren's new Communications Centre (top) was slightly more imposing than the MP4-17; Sato, Salo, Bernoldi and some sand (above)

IRVINE, NEVER SLOW WITH A REJOINDER, HIT BACK: "I MIGHT ALWAYS BE OLDER THAN RUBENS, BUT I'LL NEVER BE AS UGLY"

the Jags, the first pit stops were due. This was Barrichello's chance and he was furious when Eddie Irvine let the Williams by into the first chicane but only pulled grudgingly out of the Ferrari's way at Tosa. Rubens gave him the middle finger as he went by.

"He is the one who talks so much about etiquette during drivers' briefings," Rubens said, "so it's odd that he should hold me up. It was just silly, but he's getting old…" Irvine, never slow with a rejoinder, hit back: "I might always be older than him, but I'll never be as ugly." Calm down, children!

Barrichello lost more than a second to Schuey Jnr's Williams while Eddie suffered a possible spot of car envy. Michael had just broken the lap record with the lead Ferrari a couple of laps earlier and now, with some clear air, Rubens lowered it further. He was back on Ralf's gearbox before the Williams headed for its first stop, ran further, drove a storming "in" lap and emerged in second place. That was it. Game over.

Williams-BMW and Michelin might have won at Imola a year ago, but this was one of the worst days the tyre firm's competition competition director Pierre Dupasquier could remember. He said what most others were thinking: "Our cars performed exactly as we expected them to, but the Ferraris…"

THERE WERE ONLY 14 CARS ON THE GRID FOR the San Marino GP because the sport was in the throes of a political maelstrom. Members of the Formula One Constructors Association were at loggerheads with the authorities and 10 teams boycotted the race. But, hey, two of the cars that turned up were red so the place was packed.

The Renault RE30Bs of René Arnoux and Alain Prost qualified ahead of Gilles Villeneuve and Didier Pironi (above) in their Ferrari 126 C2s, although Prost picked up a misfire and soon retired from the race.

Arnoux v Ferrari, then. The top three circulated together until lap 44, when the Renault blew up and Villeneuve assumed the lead. Such had been the pace, however, that he wasn't confident about having enough fuel to go the distance.

Nor was the team, which ordered him to back off. He did… then Pironi passed him and sped up.

Perplexed, Gilles fought back before easing off again. Then his team-mate swept by once more. On the penultimate lap Villeneuve moved to the front and assumed that common sense would prevail. He had been the team's faster driver all weekend – by 1.3 seconds in qualifying – and was leading after Arnoux retired. By rights victory was his. Pironi had been playing to the crowd, surely? A man of honour, Villeneuve had no inkling that he was about to be suckered for keeps.

But Pironi duly zipped past and Villeneuve vowed never again to speak to him. Nor would he. Two weeks later he died at Zolder while trying to beat his team-mate's best practice time. One of the fastest men in F1 history was gone.

BRITAIN'S BEST-SELLING SINGLES… WHEN GILLES VILLENEUVE WAS DUPED	
1 JOAN JETT AND THE BLACKHEARTS	I Love Rock'n'Roll
2 THE GO-GOS	We Got The Beat
3 VANGELIS	Chariots Of Fire
4 J GEILS BAND	Freeze-Frame
5 RICK SPRINGFIELD	Don't Talk To Strangers

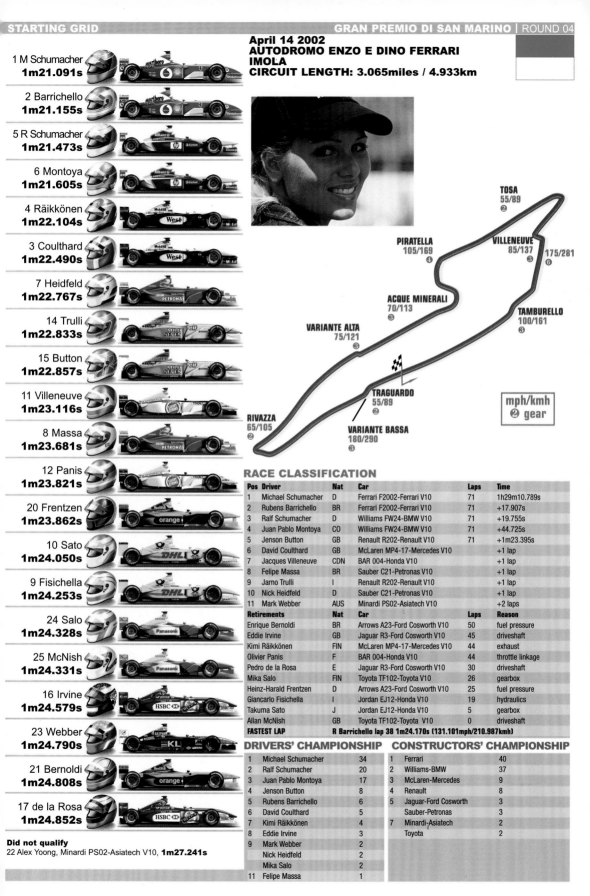

April 14 2002
AUTODROMO ENZO E DINO FERRARI
IMOLA
CIRCUIT LENGTH: 3.065miles / 4.933km

Starting Grid

1 M Schumacher — **1m21.091s**
2 Barrichello — **1m21.155s**
5 R Schumacher — **1m21.473s**
6 Montoya — **1m21.605s**
4 Räikkönen — **1m22.104s**
3 Coulthard — **1m22.490s**
7 Heidfeld — **1m22.767s**
14 Trulli — **1m22.833s**
15 Button — **1m22.857s**
11 Villeneuve — **1m23.116s**
8 Massa — **1m23.681s**
12 Panis — **1m23.821s**
20 Frentzen — **1m23.862s**
10 Sato — **1m24.050s**
9 Fisichella — **1m24.253s**
24 Salo — **1m24.328s**
25 McNish — **1m24.331s**
16 Irvine — **1m24.579s**
23 Webber — **1m24.790s**
21 Bernoldi — **1m24.808s**
17 de la Rosa — **1m24.852s**

Did not qualify
22 Alex Yoong, Minardi PS02-Asiatech V10, **1m27.241s**

Circuit labels
TOSA 55/89 ②
PIRATELLA 105/169 ①
VILLENEUVE 85/137 ③
175/281 ⑥
ACQUE MINERALI 70/113 ③
TAMBURELLO 100/161 ③
VARIANTE ALTA 75/121 ③
TRAGUARDO 55/89 ②
RIVAZZA 65/105 ②
VARIANTE BASSA 180/290 ③

mph/kmh ② gear

RACE CLASSIFICATION

Pos	Driver	Nat	Car	Laps	Time
1	Michael Schumacher	D	Ferrari F2002-Ferrari V10	71	1h29m10.789s
2	Rubens Barrichello	BR	Ferrari F2002-Ferrari V10	71	+17.907s
3	Ralf Schumacher	D	Williams FW24-BMW V10	71	+19.755s
4	Juan Pablo Montoya	CO	Williams FW24-BMW V10	71	+44.725s
5	Jenson Button	GB	Renault R202-Renault V10	71	+1m23.395s
6	David Coulthard	GB	McLaren MP4-17-Mercedes V10		+1 lap
7	Jacques Villeneuve	CDN	BAR 004-Honda V10		+1 lap
8	Felipe Massa	BR	Sauber C21-Petronas V10		+1 lap
9	Jarno Trulli	I	Renault R202-Renault V10		+1 lap
10	Nick Heidfeld	D	Sauber C21-Petronas V10		+1 lap
11	Mark Webber	AUS	Minardi PS02-Asiatech V10		+2 laps

Retirements	Nat	Car	Laps	Reason
Enrique Bernoldi	BR	Arrows A23-Ford Cosworth V10	50	fuel pressure
Eddie Irvine	GB	Jaguar R3-Ford Cosworth V10	45	driveshaft
Kimi Räikkönen	FIN	McLaren MP4-17-Mercedes V10	44	exhaust
Olivier Panis	F	BAR 004-Honda V10	44	throttle linkage
Pedro de la Rosa	E	Jaguar R3-Ford Cosworth V10	30	driveshaft
Mika Salo	FIN	Toyota TF102-Toyota V10	26	gearbox
Heinz-Harald Frentzen	D	Arrows A23-Ford Cosworth V10	25	fuel pressure
Giancarlo Fisichella	I	Jordan EJ12-Honda V10	19	hydraulics
Takuma Sato	J	Jordan EJ12-Honda V10	5	gearbox
Allan McNish	GB	Toyota TF102-Toyota V10	0	driveshaft

FASTEST LAP R Barrichello lap 38 1m24.170s (131.101mph/210.987kmh)

DRIVERS' CHAMPIONSHIP

	Driver	Pts
1	Michael Schumacher	34
2	Ralf Schumacher	20
3	Juan Pablo Montoya	17
4	Jenson Button	8
5	Rubens Barrichello	6
6	David Coulthard	5
7	Kimi Räikkönen	4
8	Eddie Irvine	3
9	Mark Webber	2
	Nick Heidfeld	2
	Mika Salo	2
11	Felipe Massa	1

CONSTRUCTORS' CHAMPIONSHIP

	Constructor	Pts
1	Ferrari	40
2	Williams-BMW	37
3	McLaren-Mercedes	9
4	Renault	8
5	Jaguar-Ford Cosworth	3
	Sauber-Petronas	3
7	Minardi-Asiatech	2
	Toyota	2

GRAN PREMIO MARLBORO DE ESPAÑA

BARCELONA IS TRADITIONALLY FERRARI
TERRITORY. AFTER IMOLA THAT COULD MEAN
ONLY ONE THING

SPANISH STROLL: evidence of art director Ryan Baptiste
having become bored choosing shots of Michael
Schumacher (left), although he manages to squeeze
the German in on a postage-stamp scale (above,
with Montoya and Coulthard) after another easy win

ONCE AGAIN RUBENS WAS PUSHING MICHAEL HARD FOR
pole position. After two runs Barrichello was on top and Schumacher
looked rattled.

"I'm actually enjoying the challenge," the world champion said with
a grin after carving a huge chunk from his previous best time to claim
top spot once again. Assuredly, though, Barrichello was able to offer
him a sterner examination in the latest Ferrari than he had in the
previous model. One theory is that a change to the traction control
system benefited Rubens more than Michael.

But as the green flag waved at the start of the final formation lap, the
poor Brazilian went nowhere because he was unable to engage first
gear as his team-mate led away. His elimination left Schuey with just
one concern – beating his younger brother's Williams to the first
corner. With that successfully accomplished, he disappeared for the
afternoon in a race all his own.

Juan Pablo Montoya tucked in behind Ralf and led a McLaren-cum-
Renault string quartet comprising Kimi Räikkönen, Jenson Button,
David Coulthard and Jarno Trulli. The Saubers were next, Nick
Heidfeld leading Felipe Massa, with Heinz-Harald Frentzen's Arrows

SCOT SHARP: Coulthard (below) took third; F1
boss Bernie Ecclestone hoping to avoid Martin
Brundle during his grid walk (top); possibly not real
mechanics (above)

completing the top six. This was a fine performance. Arrows had done precious little in the way of testing but was starting to make the similarly-powered Jaguars look daft.

Räikkönen lasted just three laps before his rear wing parted company with his MP4-17 on the front straight. It was not the first such drama of the weekend and pre-race the field had been reduced to 20 when Minardi boss Paul Stoddart opted to withdraw his team (see right).

Schumacher Jnr had a couple of seconds in hand on team-mate Montoya at their respective first fuel stops on laps 24 and 25, but when Juan Pablo started to edge closer, Ralf ran wide at Turn Nine and damaged a barge board. Cursing himself, he dived back into the pits for repairs and a fairly lengthy stop, although ultimately his engine blew on the last lap anyway.

There was more pit drama for Williams during Montoya's second stop when chief mechanic Carl Gaden put down his "stop" lollipop before alerting Montoya that the refuelling hose wasn't yet detached. Juan Pablo was already on his way and his left-front wheel pinned Gaden's foot to the Barcelona pit lane. Luckily Montoya still had his hand on the clutch and managed to stop. What could have been very nasty required just an ice-pack for Gaden, who was able to cheer his man on the podium half an hour later.

ARROWS HAD DONE PRECIOUS LITTLE IN THE WAY OF TESTING BUT WAS STARTING TO MAKE THE SIMILARLY-POWERED JAGUARS LOOK DAFT

WING GYP

KIMI RÄIKKÖNEN RETIRED EARLY FROM THE Spanish Grand Prix because his McLaren's rear wing flew skywards on the main straight, but both Minardis were long since packed away by then, following similar problems.

The front wing on Mark Webber's car broke and lodged itself under the nose as the Aussie nudged 200mph past the pits during Saturday morning's free practice. Briefly, both front wheels were off the ground. It looked more dramatic on the TV monitors than Webber reported from the cockpit.

"We brought two different wings and after Mark's incident we reverted to our original," team boss Paul Stoddart said. But that did not stop Alex Yoong having another breakage when he ran wide out of Turn 13 in qualifying (above). The Minardi composite men in Faenza worked through the night to produce reinforced wings for Sunday. At such times owning an airline definitely helps.

In the warm-up, though, Webber had yet another failure – this time at the rear. He was adjusting the engine mapping at the time and thought this might have been responsible for the little jink he felt. He was rudely alerted to the lack of rear downforce when he braked for the Esses and his car promptly swapped ends.

Barcelona imposes high aerodynamic loadings and withdrawal was the only sensible option.

When a McLaren broke it was a little different, however, and the team didn't call David Coulthard in after Räikkönen's failure. Team principal Ron Dennis said: "Within less than a minute we were able to look at our database and confirm that the wing assembly on David's car was effectively new. We were convinced that there was no risk."

McLaren telemetry showed that downforce figures peaked when cars passed the new grandstand opposite the pits, because it acted as a sort of wind tunnel. That might have contributed to the failures, but they were more likely to have been the result of additional loadings caused by traction control and added grip.

TRACTION MAN: Button's grippy Renault keeps Coulthard at bay. Inset, Frentzen – still fired up two weeks short of his 35th birthday

SAUBER WAS BUSY POURING EGG DOWN THE FACES OF MANY TEAMS WITH FULL MANUFACTURER BACKING

Ralf's tribulations meant that Button was promoted to third as Renault continued to look stronger. At the first round of stops he maintained his advantage over Coulthard but the team spotted an imminent hydraulic problem. They radioed Jenson and suggested he should be able to make it to the end but he was already hampered by understeer.

"It was getting worse and worse until I had my arms completely crossed out of some corners," he explained.

Coulthard took full advantage: "I could see him having a few problems in the last corner and I managed to get close enough to outbrake him at the end of the straight," the Scot said. Button's hydraulic problems worsened, Jarno Trulli was troubled by a throttle problem and neither Renault scored.

Step forward Sauber-Petronas. The Swiss outfit has Ferrari engines but it pays for them and was busy pouring egg down the faces of many with full manufacturer backing. The team doesn't have a name driver, no disrespect to Heidfeld, and tests relatively infrequently. Heidfeld ran with McLaren and Renault early on and finished a comfortable fourth, just 12s ahead of rookie team-mate Massa. The top three teams might have lost a car each, but this was still a fine effort from Peter Sauber's crew.

Frentzen put Massa under tremendous pressure in the closing stages but the little Brazilian refused to be pushed into a mistake. It was a good enough tussle to keep Michael Schumacher amused, the champion easing back to observe from a distance without bothering to put the protagonists a lap down.

"I had a big lead and I saw no point in getting involved or interrupting their fight," Schumacher said. "Besides, I was enjoying it."

FLASHBACK

May 12 1968. Jarama, Spain

LOTUS SORELY needed a pick-me-up. Little more than a month before the Spanish GP the team had lost its talismanic leader Jim Clark, who crashed fatally during a Formula Two race at Hockenheim, Germany.

And then there was Mike Spence, nominated to take over what would have been Clark's Lotus in the Indianapolis 500. The underrated Englishman had just succumbed to injuries sustained while testing for America's biggest race.

Spain's first world championship F1 event since 1954 could hardly have fallen at a more sombre time. What's more, there was political unrest beforehand: the drivers wanted safety modifications made to the circuit and they refused to countenance entries from a couple of local optimists (Jorge de Bagration and Alex Soler-Roig in a brace of Lola T100s, which were designed for F2 rather than grands prix). When the meeting finally began there were only 14 cars in the paddock – and Jack Brabham failed to start after blowing an engine in practice.

Graham Hill (above) qualified the lone works Lotus 49 sixth and worked his way up to fourth after a handful of laps. Then Jean-Pierre Beltoise (Matra MS10) pitted to have an over-tight oil pipe union washer freed and Pedro Rodriguez (BRM P133) crashed out. Hill lay second, but Chris Amon (Ferrari 312) was a long way up the road and pulling away. As always when he found himself in a position of apparent invincibility, however, Amon hit trouble. Lap 58, broken fuel pump: another unjust footnote in an ultimately winless GP career.

Hill quietly slipped through to take the lead and, 32 laps later, the chequered flag. It wasn't a great race but for Lotus the victory could not have been more timely.

BRITAIN'S BEST-SELLING SINGLES... WHEN GRAHAM HILL GAVE LOTUS A LIFT	
1 LOUIS ARMSTRONG	Wonderful World
2 SMALL FACES	Lazy Sunday
3 ENGELBERT HUMPERDINCK	Man Without Love
4 1910 FRUITGUM CO	Simon Says
5 GARY PUCKETT AND THE UNION GAP	Young Girl

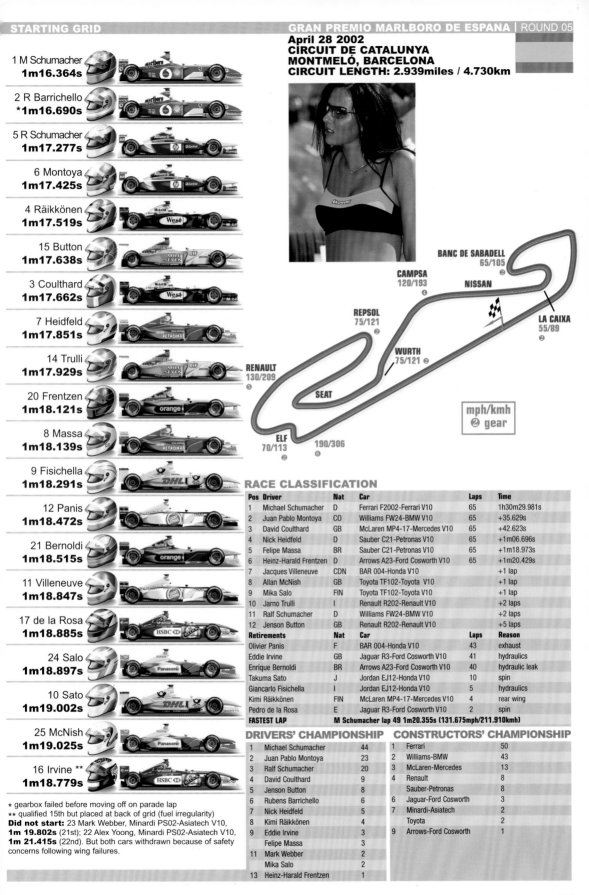

April 28 2002
CIRCUIT DE CATALUNYA
MONTMELÓ, BARCELONA
CIRCUIT LENGTH: 2.939miles / 4.730km

Starting Grid

1 M Schumacher — 1m16.364s
2 R Barrichello — *1m16.690s
5 R Schumacher — 1m17.277s
6 Montoya — 1m17.425s
4 Räikkönen — 1m17.519s
15 Button — 1m17.638s
3 Coulthard — 1m17.662s
7 Heidfeld — 1m17.851s
14 Trulli — 1m17.929s
20 Frentzen — 1m18.121s
8 Massa — 1m18.139s
9 Fisichella — 1m18.291s
12 Panis — 1m18.472s
21 Bernoldi — 1m18.515s
11 Villeneuve — 1m18.847s
17 de la Rosa — 1m18.885s
24 Salo — 1m18.897s
10 Sato — 1m19.002s
25 McNish — 1m19.025s
16 Irvine ** — 1m18.779s

* gearbox failed before moving off on parade lap
** qualified 15th but placed at back of grid (fuel irregularity)
Did not start: 23 Mark Webber, Minardi PS02-Asiatech V10,
1m 19.802s (21st); 22 Alex Yoong, Minardi PS02-Asiatech V10,
1m 21.415s (22nd). But both cars withdrawn because of safety
concerns following wing failures.

Circuit sections:
BANC DE SABADELL 65/105 ②
CAMPSA 120/193 ①
NISSAN
REPSOL 75/121 ②
LA CAIXA 55/89 ②
WURTH 75/121 ②
RENAULT 130/209 ⑥
SEAT
ELF 70/113 ②   190/306 ⑥

mph/kmh ② gear

RACE CLASSIFICATION

Pos	Driver	Nat	Car	Laps	Time
1	Michael Schumacher	D	Ferrari F2002-Ferrari V10	65	1h30m29.981s
2	Juan Pablo Montoya	CO	Williams FW24-BMW V10	65	+35.629s
3	David Coulthard	GB	McLaren MP4-17-Mercedes V10	65	+42.623s
4	Nick Heidfeld	D	Sauber C21-Petronas V10	65	+1m06.696s
5	Felipe Massa	BR	Sauber C21-Petronas V10	65	+1m18.973s
6	Heinz-Harald Frentzen	D	Arrows A23-Ford Cosworth V10	65	+1m20.429s
7	Jacques Villeneuve	CDN	BAR 004-Honda V10		+1 lap
8	Allan McNish	GB	Toyota TF102-Toyota V10		+1 lap
9	Mika Salo	FIN	Toyota TF102-Toyota V10		+1 lap
10	Jarno Trulli	I	Renault R202-Renault V10		+2 laps
11	Ralf Schumacher	D	Williams FW24-BMW V10		+2 laps
12	Jenson Button	GB	Renault R202-Renault V10		+5 laps

Retirements		Nat	Car	Laps	Reason
Olivier Panis		F	BAR 004-Honda V10	43	exhaust
Eddie Irvine		GB	Jaguar R3-Ford Cosworth V10	41	hydraulics
Enrique Bernoldi		BR	Arrows A23-Ford Cosworth V10	40	hydraulic leak
Takuma Sato		J	Jordan EJ12-Honda V10	10	spin
Giancarlo Fisichella		I	Jordan EJ12-Honda V10	5	hydraulics
Kimi Räikkönen		FIN	McLaren MP4-17-Mercedes V10	4	rear wing
Pedro de la Rosa		E	Jaguar R3-Ford Cosworth V10	2	spin

FASTEST LAP   M Schumacher lap 49 1m20.355s (131.675mph/211.910kmh)

DRIVERS' CHAMPIONSHIP

1	Michael Schumacher	44
2	Juan Pablo Montoya	23
3	Ralf Schumacher	20
4	David Coulthard	9
5	Jenson Button	8
6	Rubens Barrichello	6
7	Nick Heidfeld	5
8	Kimi Räikkönen	4
9	Eddie Irvine	3
	Felipe Massa	3
11	Mark Webber	2
	Mika Salo	2
13	Heinz-Harald Frentzen	1

CONSTRUCTORS' CHAMPIONSHIP

1	Ferrari	50
2	Williams-BMW	43
3	McLaren-Mercedes	13
4	Renault	8
	Sauber-Petronas	8
6	Jaguar-Ford Cosworth	3
7	Minardi-Asiatech	2
	Toyota	2
9	Arrows-Ford Cosworth	1

GROSSER A1 PREIS VON ÖSTERREICH

FERRARI'S SECOND ONE-TWO IN THREE RACES MIGHT HAVE
DELIGHTED THE ACCOUNTANTS IN MARANELLO, BUT AMONG
THE TRADITIONALLY BACCHANALIAN AUSTRIAN FANS IT WAS
A CASE OF BOOS RATHER THAN BOOZE

PIECES IN OUR TIME: Sato's Jordan fell to bits after Heidfeld reversed into
him (below). Meanwhile, the manner in which Ferrari stage-managed the
result shouldn't have perplexed Schuey Jnr (left). Williams asked him to
move aside once or twice for Montoya in 2001, but unfortunately his radio
was always on the blink.

UNLUCKY STRIKE: above from left, Villeneuve snags Frentzen in the Turn Two traffic jam on the opening lap; the French-Canadian later got a grandstand view of Felipe Massa being, er, Felipe Massa; Montoya en route to third. Pretty sight (main shot): Fisichella and some trees. Not a pretty sight (below): feeling a bit uncomfortable about team orders and all those booing Austrians, are we?

YOU'D SEEN IT SO OFTEN BEFORE BUT STILL YOU WERE shocked when it happened. It wasn't the first time a Ferrari driver had been asked to move over for Michael Schumacher but Austria stuck in the throat. Rubens Barrichello backed right off and handed the race on a plate to Michael with the chequered flag in sight. Even Schuey was embarrassed. He ushered Rubens up onto the podium's top step, confusing Austrian big cheeses presenting the trophies. A heinous crime, apparently.

The crowd booed and, in the press room, even the media were upset. This was a novelty among a group of people who've seen most things. Cynical bordering on the fraudulent, said a rival team principal.

A year earlier Rubens had been required to do likewise. Same race, same place, same deal. So what was the difference?

Quite simply, in 2001 Rubens was ahead of Michael only because Schumacher had been assisted off the circuit by JP Montoya trying to prove his manhood. Rubens fretted about it then, which was hard to fathom. As we said in *Grand Prix Year 2001/02*: "The time for him to get the hump about moving out of Michael's way is the weekend he outqualifies and outraces him."

Which, of course, is precisely what he did this time. Last year we were talking second place, not a win, and this year the situation was

very different. Such was Ferrari's superiority that nobody was offering a realistic title challenge to Schumacher. And Rubens was genuinely quicker on this occasion. He had qualified on pole position and led the race from start to within inches of the finish.

The timing could have been better for F1, too. Already there were mutterings about viewing figures heading south and the word "boring" was starting to cross a few too many lips.

Rubens handled himself with great dignity. It was his wife Silvana's birthday, he pointed out, and it would have been nice to take home the winner's trophy. Which is why Michael gave it to him.

"The team asked me to move over and of course I did," he said. "I have stopped crying about this type of thing and I'm going through a good time in my life. I think I am a better person and a better driver and this will not affect my motivation."

To be fair to Michael, he didn't like it either, although Jacques Villeneuve was quick to point out that he was happy enough to accept the 10 points without having the balls to stand alone on the top step of the podium.

"I don't take any pleasure from this," Schumacher said. "I enjoyed the race except for the last hundred metres. Only at the very end was I called on the radio and told Rubens would move over. He did a

IT WASN'T THE FIRST TIME THAT A FERRARI DRIVER HAD BEEN ASKED TO MOVE OVER FOR MICHAEL SCHUMACHER BUT AUSTRIA STUCK IN THE THROAT

BRICKBAT OUT OF HELL

SHORTLY AFTER THE AUSTRIAN GP IT WAS announced that Ferrari would be called before the FIA World Council to explain its actions.

Some even suggested that there would be draconian penalties for bringing the sport into disrepute. What a load of old nonsense.

Someone with more sense, who's been around a bit, scratched his head and said: "I don't really see what the fuss is all about. Disrepute? If everyone else is tossing so much that Ferrari can write the script at will, it's not them that should be facing the charges"

In the end, Ferrari was fined for a serious breach of podium protocol – ie Barrichello and Schuey swapping places hit for half a million bucks for upsetting an Austrian in a blazer, basically.

Team orders aren't exactly a new concept.

Ferrari technical director Ross Brawn said: "It was very tough on Rubens because he's had such bad luck this year. But there's a history of this sort of thing in motor racing. Remember Mario Andretti and Ronnie Peterson at Lotus in 1978? The fact is that for three seasons from 1997 Ferrari lost the championship at the last race. After the first two, I remember us sitting there at Jerez and Suzuka asking ourselves whether we could have done anything differently. We are not conceited enough to think that we have a big enough margin over our competitors to forget about our principles. In 1999 Michael broke his leg. Anything can happen in motor racing."

At Ferrari in 1979, Gilles Villeneuve had to play second fiddle to Jody Scheckter when he was quicker, which must have been a lot harder than accepting that you are not quite as good as M Schumacher, but no one complained. There have been many other recent instances of team orders, too, but it seems Schuey has unique magnetism when it comes to attracting brickbats.

TYRED AND EMOTIONAL: Nick Heidfeld was able to release himself from the wreckage after his shunt with Sato, but he was shaken up nonetheless

NICK HEIDFELD LOST CONTROL OF HIS SAUBER UNDER BRAKING AND SPUN BACKWARDS INTO TAKUMA SATO. VERY HARD

superb job and outpaced me all weekend. I feel very sorry for him."

But not sorry enough to roll up behind and follow him across the line?

"I thought about this for a moment but I didn't have much time." Schuey said. "I saw him back off and I backed off, but then he backed off even more. It was a team decision and I think it was wrong."

In a way it was as unfortunate for Michael as it was for Rubens. Like the late, great Ayrton Senna, Schumacher gives his all week-in, week-out and performs at an inspirational level that is a privilege to witness. Yet there he was, having to listen to dim suggestions that his fifth championship would be worthless.

Ferrari again issued the party line, which is that it spends a great deal of money trying to win the championship and would look extremely stupid if it lost through letting its number two beat its number one.

"In 1999," Schumacher said, "Mika Häkkinen almost lost his title because McLaren let David Coulthard win at Spa. This is a team sport, is it not?"

The Ferrari ructions buried all other news. For the record, that included two Safety Car periods. First for a lurid spin by Panis on the front straight courtesy of a seized Honda, then immediately after the restart because Nick Heidfeld lost his Sauber under braking and spun backwards into Takuma Sato. Very hard. Although sore, the young Japanese was happily fit to race a classic Lotus 49 in Monaco the following weekend.

The Safety Car periods played into the hands of a one-stopping Montoya, on the harder Michelin, and he beat Schuey Jnr for the second successive race. Giancarlo Fisichella took Jordan's first points of 2002 and David Coulthard was sixth. Ferrari, though, had taken the sport from the back pages to the front.

FLASHBACK
August 14 1977. Österreichring, Austria

NIKI LAUDA'S SECOND WORLD TITLE IN 1977 owed as much to stealth as to speed.

The Austrian won only three of 17 races in his elegant Ferrari 312 T2. Jody Scheckter (Wolf WR1) and James Hunt (McLaren M26) were just as successful in terms of victories – and Mario Andretti (Lotus 78) outscored them all, with four.

No one, however, could match Lauda for consistency: he scored points in 12 of the 15 races he started and was on the podium in all but two of those. It was one thing standing alongside Hunt, Scheckter or Andretti, however, but Alan Jones?

At the time the Australian world-champ-to-be was driving for the unfancied Shadow team (above). Recruited earlier in the season to replace Tom Pryce, who had been killed at Kyalami, he had yet to finish better than fifth.

Here he qualified his DN8 14th and his progress on a damp-but-drying track was modest in the opening stages of the race. He was running 10th on lap seven when he began to let others in on a little secret: that day the DN8 was dynamite. In the next nine laps he carved his way up to second – and most of it was progress made the hard way. Early leader Andretti blew up and his team-mate Gunnar Nilsson pitted to switch from wets to slicks. The rest? Jones just drove around them.

That looked to be his lot, mind, because Hunt, driving beautifully, was well in control. With 11 laps to go, however, the Englishman's Cosworth DFV exploded. Jones strolled home more than 20 seconds clear of local favourite Lauda to score Shadow's first – and last – GP success.

BRITAIN'S BEST-SELLING SINGLES... WHEN ALAN JONES MADE US SAY "WHAT?" ON HEARING THE SPORTS NEWS	
1 BROTHERHOOD OF MAN	Angelo
2 DONNA SUMMER	I Feel Love
3 SHOWADDYWADDY	You Got What It Takes
4 FLOATERS	Float On
5 BONEY M	Ma Baker

May 12 2002
A1-RING
SPIELBERG
CIRCUIT LENGTH: 2.688miles / 4.326km

2 Barrichello
1m08.082s

5 R Schumacher
1m08.364s

1 M Schumacher
1m08.704s

6 Montoya
1m09.118s

7 Heidfeld
1m09.129s

4 Räikkönen
1m09.154s

8 Massa
1m09.228s

3 Coulthard
1m09.335s

12 Panis
1m09.561s

24 Salo
1m09.661s

20 Frentzen
1m09.671s

21 Bernoldi
1m09.723s

15 Button
1m09.780s

25 McNish
1m09.818s

9 Fisichella
1m09.901s

14 Trulli
1m09.980s

11 Villeneuve
1m10.051s

10 Sato
1m10.058s

17 de la Rosa
1m10.533s

16 Irvine
1m10.741s

23 Webber
1m11.388s

22 Yoong
1m12.336s

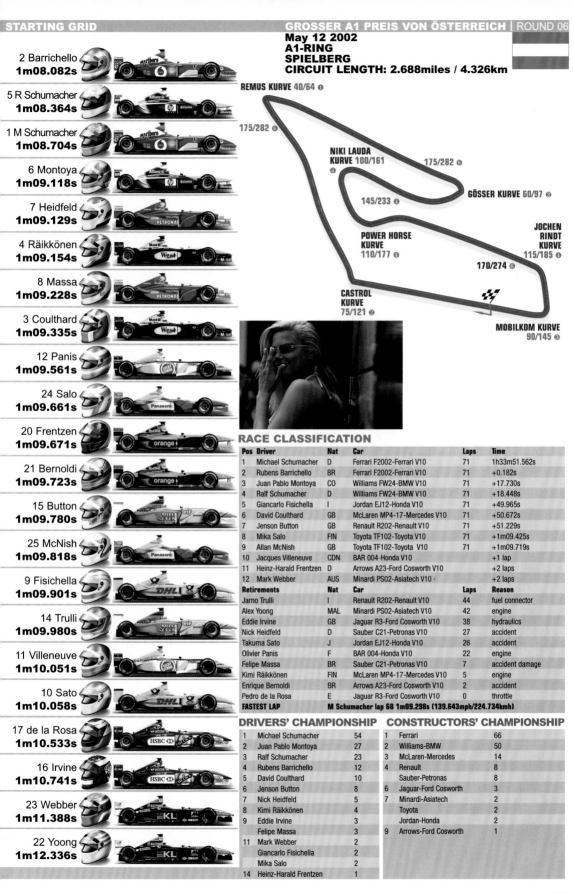

REMUS KURVE 40/64
175/282
NIKI LAUDA KURVE 100/161
175/282
145/233
GÖSSER KURVE 60/97
POWER HORSE KURVE 110/177
JOCHEN RINDT KURVE 115/185
170/274
CASTROL KURVE 75/121
MOBILKOM KURVE 90/145

RACE CLASSIFICATION

Pos	Driver	Nat	Car	Laps	Time
1	Michael Schumacher	D	Ferrari F2002-Ferrari V10	71	1h33m51.562s
2	Rubens Barrichello	BR	Ferrari F2002-Ferrari V10	71	+0.182s
3	Juan Pablo Montoya	CO	Williams FW24-BMW V10	71	+17.730s
4	Ralf Schumacher	D	Williams FW24-BMW V10	71	+18.448s
5	Giancarlo Fisichella	I	Jordan EJ12-Honda V10	71	+49.965s
6	David Coulthard	GB	McLaren MP4-17-Mercedes V10	71	+50.672s
7	Jenson Button	GB	Renault R202-Renault V10	71	+51.229s
8	Mika Salo	FIN	Toyota TF102-Toyota V10	71	+1m09.425s
9	Allan McNish	GB	Toyota TF102-Toyota V10	71	+1m09.719s
10	Jacques Villeneuve	CDN	BAR 004-Honda V10		+1 lap
11	Heinz-Harald Frentzen	D	Arrows A23-Ford Cosworth V10		+2 laps
12	Mark Webber	AUS	Minardi PS02-Asiatech V10		+2 laps

Retirements	Nat	Car	Laps	Reason
Jarno Trulli	I	Renault R202-Renault V10	44	fuel connector
Alex Yoong	MAL	Minardi PS02-Asiatech V10	42	engine
Eddie Irvine	GB	Jaguar R3-Ford Cosworth V10	38	hydraulics
Nick Heidfeld	D	Sauber C21-Petronas V10	27	accident
Takuma Sato	J	Jordan EJ12-Honda V10	26	accident
Olivier Panis	F	BAR 004-Honda V10	22	engine
Felipe Massa	BR	Sauber C21-Petronas V10	7	accident damage
Kimi Räikkönen	FIN	McLaren MP4-17-Mercedes V10	5	engine
Enrique Bernoldi	BR	Arrows A23-Ford Cosworth V10	2	accident
Pedro de la Rosa	E	Jaguar R3-Ford Cosworth V10	0	throttle
FASTEST LAP		M Schumacher lap 68 1m09.298s (139.643mph/224.734kmh)		

DRIVERS' CHAMPIONSHIP

1	Michael Schumacher	54
2	Juan Pablo Montoya	27
3	Ralf Schumacher	23
4	Rubens Barrichello	12
5	David Coulthard	10
6	Jenson Button	8
7	Nick Heidfeld	5
8	Kimi Räikkönen	4
9	Eddie Irvine	3
	Felipe Massa	3
11	Mark Webber	2
	Giancarlo Fisichella	2
	Mika Salo	2
14	Heinz-Harald Frentzen	1

CONSTRUCTORS' CHAMPIONSHIP

1	Ferrari	66
2	Williams-BMW	50
3	McLaren-Mercedes	14
4	Renault	8
	Sauber-Petronas	8
6	Jaguar-Ford Cosworth	3
7	Minardi-Asiatech	2
	Toyota	2
	Jordan-Honda	2
9	Arrows-Ford Cosworth	1

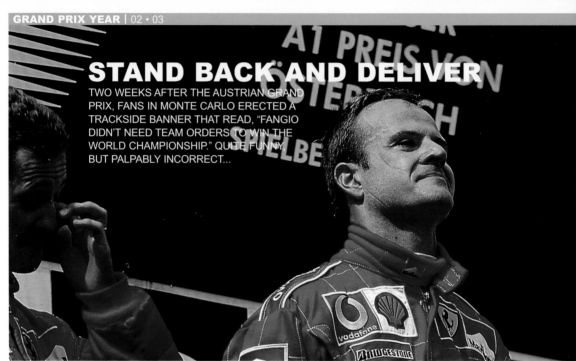

STAND BACK AND DELIVER

TWO WEEKS AFTER THE AUSTRIAN GRAND PRIX, FANS IN MONTE CARLO ERECTED A TRACKSIDE BANNER THAT READ, "FANGIO DIDN'T NEED TEAM ORDERS TO WIN THE WORLD CHAMPIONSHIP." QUITE FUNNY, BUT PALPABLY INCORRECT...

DO THE SHUFFLE: Schuey and Rubens looking ever so slightly shifty in Austria, where they were roundly booed after switching positions a) on the track and b) on the podium

EVERYONE APART from Ferrari appeared outraged by what the Scuderia did in Austria. Point was, however, that the team deserved criticism for style rather than substance. When Rubens Barrichello ceded

to team orders a few centimetres from the line Ferrari was simply maintaining a long-standing motor sport tradition. It just did so somewhat gracelessly.

And for the information of our banner-waving mates in Monte Carlo (above), Juan Manuel Fangio was involved in just such stage-management. Indeed, the Argentine legend didn't merely rely on his team-mates' occasional subservience, he sometimes helped himself to their cars mid-race, in the days when such changeovers were permitted. It was one of the privileges of greatness, which was something he had earned. Arguably, you could say

the same about Schumacher. If only he could bring himself to handle such occasions with dignity rather than pious claptrap. The suggestion – his own – that he could not disobey team orders in Austria was preposterous. What was Ferrari going to do? Summon him to a crisis meeting in Maranello on Monday morning and issue a P45? Confiscate his company 360 and issue him with a Fiat Punto?

This was a delicate, but not unusual, racing situation that was very badly handled. Here are a few others about which rather less fuss has been made.

RACE: FRENCH GP
VENUE: REIMS
DATE: JULY 1 1951
BENEFICIARY: JUAN MANUEL FANGIO
GUINEA PIG: LUIGI FAGIOLI
CAR: ALFA ROMEO 159B
CIRCUMSTANCES:
The fourth of eight rounds in Fangio's first world title season. The Argentine ace qualified on pole, but hit technical trouble early on. Fagioli was running third when he made his mid-race pit stop... at which point Alfa Romeo's management turfed him out of the car and gave it to Fangio, who went on to win after team-mate Giuseppe Farina slowed with magneto trouble. Fagioli took over Fangio's original car, more than 20 laps behind by now, and finished 11th. Afterwards the 53-year-old had a ripe old tantrum and stropped away never to race in F1 again.

RACE: ITALIAN GP
VENUE: MONZA
DATE: SEPTEMBER 2 1956
BENEFICIARY: JUAN MANUEL FANGIO
GUINEA PIG: PETER COLLINS
CAR: LANCIA-FERRARI D50
CIRCUMSTANCES: Earlier in the season Collins had done Fangio a favour by handing over his car in Monaco, where the

pair shared second place, but in Italy the circumstances were rather more dramatic. Here, the Englishman had an outside chance of taking the world title, which was amplified when Fangio suffered a broken steering arm. It was anticipated that the Argentine would take over second-placed Luigi Musso's car, but the Italian stayed put after his scheduled stop. Collins was on course to become Britain's first world champ when he pitted to check his tyres with 15 laps to go. Ferrari asked if he would hand over his car to Fangio and Collins immediately agreed. Stirling Moss won the race in his Maserati, but a share of second place was enough to give Fangio his third straight title – and a fourth in all. Collins believed, with reason, that he had the potential to win the championship in future, but an accident at the Nürburgring in 1958 meant he didn't live to realise it.

Scheckter 8-7), but in many races Villeneuve had the edge. His word being his bond, he chose not to exercise his advantage. When it rained heavily during the opening qualifying session for the United States GP East at Watkins Glen, Villeneuve was more than 10 seconds per lap quicker than Scheckter... Enough said.

RACE: BRAZILIAN GP
VENUE: RIO DE JANEIRO
DATE: MARCH 29 1981
INTENDED BENEFICIARY: ALAN JONES
INTENDED GUINEA PIG: CARLOS REUTEMANN
CAR: WILLIAMS FW07C
CIRCUMSTANCES:
Jones was reigning world champion and terrifically popular within Williams. (When David Coulthard joined the team as test driver in 1993, he assumed principals Frank Williams and Patrick Head were referring to lead driver of the day Monsieur Prost when they told him how "Alain" did things; in fact, they were harping on about Mr Jones.) Anyway, we digress... The bottom line is that Reutemann was leading in the closing stages of the race with Jones tucked in behind. The team put out constant pit signals telling Carlos to move over – and Jones, expecting his colleague to comply, sat there patiently. But Reutemann ignored all instructions and went on to win, which seems fair enough. In the same race, incidentally, the Talbot Ligier team ordered Jean-Pierre Jarier to step aside for sidekick Jacques Laffite. He did, but it only cost him sixth place rather than victory.

RACE: ALL OF THEM
VENUE: EVERYWHERE
DATE: JAN 21-OCT 7 1979
BENEFICIARY: JODY SCHECKTER
GUINEA PIG: GILLES VILLENEUVE
CAR: FERRARI 312 T4
CIRCUMSTANCES: Simple. Scheckter had a deal that gave him preferential status, Villeneuve was inherently the quicker of the two. But he was also a man of integrity. He agreed to play the team game. Jody had more experience; Gilles had time on his side. They were fairly even in terms of qualifying (Villeneuve outpaced

RACE: AUSTRALIAN GP
VENUE: MELBOURNE
DATE: MARCH 8 1998
BENEFICIARY: MIKA HÄKKINEN
GUINEA PIG: DAVID COULTHARD
CAR: McLAREN MP4/13

CIRCUMSTANCES: Benefiting from the first Adrian Newey-designed McLaren, Coulthard and Häkkinen knew they could have strolled to an easy one-two had they driven the season's opening race blindfolded. At the start of any campaign, however, reliability is paramount. Not wanting to push themselves to breaking point, the drivers agreed that whoever won the sprint to the first corner could have the race. Coulthard might have qualified second, but he was an acknowledged ace off the line and fancied his chances. On this occasion, however, Mika's judgement was even more acute. Game over... except that late in the race the Finn sped into the pit lane for reasons best known to himself and Coulthard had no option but to overtake him. Having been alerted by McLaren to the fact his team-mate was a dingbat, Coulthard subsequently did the honourable thing and waved Häkkinen back into the lead, which upset lots of Australians who had stuck a few dollars on the second-placed McLaren.

GRAND PRIX DE MONACO

THE STREETS OF MONTE
CARLO: TRADITIONALLY
THAT SPELLS MICHAEL AND
FERRARI, SO SURELY THAT
WOULD BE THE CASE
THIS YEAR? WRONG

RED BARREN: an opening spread
with remarkably little Ferrari
content, thanks to a bold gamble by
Michelin and a well-judged drive
by Coulthard, who kept the lurking
Schuey at bay (left). The Scot looks
like he needs a good shower
(above); fortunately, he only lives
five minutes away by scooter

THIS WAS A MILITARY OPERATION. WITH AN OUTSIDE chance of success if every last detail worked out.

Having your snout in front, "track position" as they like to call it, is what Monte Carlo is all about. David Coulthard's inability to pass Enrique Bernoldi's Arrows for 40-odd laps 12 months earlier sowed the seeds of Michelin's battle plan in 2002.

You wouldn't have given much for Coulthard and a McLaren MP4-17 versus Michael Schumacher and a Ferrari F2002 over 78 laps this time, but Michelin motorsport boss Pierre Dupasquier and his men had other ideas.

The softest tyre compounds of the year are used in Monaco. Speeds are relatively slow and temperatures relatively mild for the region. The cars run a bit higher too, to compensate for the bumps, manhole covers, pavements and crowns that are all part of a street circuit. You want a bit more give in the tyre, a bit more feel.

Michelin figured that if a Williams or McLaren – and preferably both – could outqualify Ferrari, then there was a chance. And so they went

CRUISE LINE IS IT ANYWAY? Monaco – not likely to be confused with Germany (above). Right, from top: Montoya fends off a predator; Sato learns the consequences of turning left in the tunnel; decent bloke-cum-hero Alex Zanardi continues to make light of his prosthetic legs, fitted after a horrific Champ Car accident in September 2001. Below, Salo flirts with the Armco

THE McLAREN WAS PAST AND THROUGH SAINTE DEVOTE UNSCATHED AND IN FRONT. THE TROOPS HAD TAKEN THE BRIDGE AND WERE IN CONTROL

RUSSELL BULGIN
1958-2002

MOTOR SPORT IS PACKED WITH HEROES BUT IT might surprise you to learn that journalism has its share, too. Russell Bulgin was one such.

I first got to know him over a cup of coffee at a harbourside bar during the build-up to the 1983 Monaco GP. It was a thrill to make the acquaintance of a man who had been such an inspiration to an aspiring writer. At university I would pore several times over his every word instead of following my tutors' instructions to cram up on the use of allegory in Edmund Spenser's *Faerie Queene*, or some similar task. Sod that when the latest edition of *Cars & Car Conversions* had just come out.

Over the years Russell (pictured with the somewhat smaller Ayrton Senna, above) became a valued associate and colleague, one who would never know the sense of pride that accompanied acceptance of his commissions, largely because I never quite got round to mentioning it. Sadly, any opportunity to do so has now gone.

Shortly after walking into the press room at this year's Monaco GP I learned that the cancer he had been fighting with dignity, resolution and good humour had claimed him. He was just 43 years old.

Russell had a knack with words and could have applied it to anything, but it was our good fortune that cars and motor sport tended to be his preferred topics. It didn't matter whether he was describing Jenson Button's goatee, the engine note of a BMW straight six or the tactile quality of the switchgear in a Skoda Octavia cabin, he always did so in a style that was equal parts authority and entertainment.

We will miss his distinctive prose. Most of all, though, we will miss a thoroughly good bloke.
Simon Arron

with an option tyre as soft as they dared. Juan Pablo Montoya duly did the business and took a fine pole. And Coulthard, crucially, pipped Michael's Ferrari to the front row.

It was now all about the first few yards.

"The software guys have worked really hard," DC revealed. "They've made some big steps and, analysing our Austrian starts, the team was confident that I would lead into the first corner."

Sure enough, Montoya had his nose in front for the first few yards, then the McLaren was past and through Sainte Devote unscathed and in front. The troops had taken the bridge and were in control. But could DC repel the enemy assault?

Of course, the boot was now on the other foot. The soft Michelin, so useful to DC on Saturday afternoon, needed nursing. Michael's Bridgestone would be more forgiving as a race tyre and potentially quicker. It was good that Montoya, in the same boat as DC, was there as a buffer. But Juan is Juan. Run too slow and you never know what he might try. So, watch the mirrors down into Mirabeau and the chicane, and keep it off the wall everywhere else.

For the first few laps DC led them around in the 1m22s bracket. But then, just seven laps in, he slowed things down to the 1m24s-1m25s range. The Michelins were graining. "I thought I was going to be in big

BLACK. IT,S THE NEW, ER, BLACK: five people about whom we know absolutely nothing, except that they seem to be quite big on dental hygiene. And sunglasses

DC HAD HIS SECOND MONTE CARLO WIN. THE TINIEST WINDOW OF OPPORTUNITY PERFECTLY EXPLOITED. MISSION ACCOMPLISHED

trouble," he explained, "but then the tyres cleaned up and came back in."

For the first time he was able to put a bit of breathing space between himself and Montoya. But then he noticed wisps of smoke. There it was as he accelerated up the hill out of Sainte Devote. And again along the harbour front. Borrowed time now, surely?

But no. There was a jammed valve to the car's auxiliary oil tank and the team was venting it via the pits-to-car telemetry. He should be okay.

Half-distance came and went. The strategy was to run relatively long. But Michael stopped on lap 44. Then Montoya blew up. Damn. That was the buffer gone. Brace yourself for the enemy counter-attack.

It came with a vengeance. Michael's first lap on new Bridgestones was comfortably the fastest of the race. DC had enjoyed a five-second cushion when the Ferrari went in but Schumacher was now in clean air and could run to his potential for the first time. He started to lap significantly faster than DC despite carrying extra weight because he had just refuelled. The battle plans didn't allow for that. That Bridgestone was some race tyre and threatened to turn the battle.

The generals reacted. DC was summoned to the pits earlier than planned, in the nick of time. He emerged with just a second in hand over the Ferrari. But here, of all places, that might as well have been a minute.

That's the way everyone thinks, at any rate. But it still meant a third of the race to run without a mistake, knowing that Michael, in a Ferrari, with a quicker race tyre, would need no second invitation. But like every other part of the plan, it was executed to perfection. There was no mistake. DC had his second Monte Carlo win. The tiniest window of opportunity perfectly exploited. Mission accomplished.

FLASHBACK

May 21 1950, Monaco
THERE WERE only seven rounds of the inaugural Formula One World Champion- ship in 1950 – and the
first two took place only eight days apart.

After the previous weekend's ground-breaking event on the wide, open expanses of Silverstone, teams trundled south to address the tighter challenge of Monte Carlo.

Juan Manuel Fangio qualified his Alfa Romeo 158 on pole position and duly led away, but while he managed to glide effortlessly through the left-hander at Tabac halfway through the opening lap, his rivals didn,t make quite such a good fist of it. It was a dry but breezy day and spray rising from the harbour was blamed for slippery conditions that caused second-placed Giuseppe Farina (Alfa Romeo) – the Silverstone winner – to lose control. Within seconds there was chaos and a chain-reaction accident took out nine of the 19 starters – Farina plus Luigi Fagioli (Alfa Romeo 158), Robert Manzon (Simca Gordini T15), Harry Schell (Cooper T12), Louis Rosier (Talbot Lago T26C), Emmanuel de Graffenried (Maserati 4CLT/48), Maurice Trintignant (Simca Gordini T15), Cuth Harrison (ERA B-type) and Franco Rol (Maserati 4CLT/48). Froilan Gonzalez (Maserati 4CLT/48) was also involved and pitted to retire with accident damage at the end of the lap.

By the time those still running approached Tabac on the second lap marshals were still working furiously to clear up the mess. Fangio, though, spotted that the crowd wasn't looking at him, even though he was leading the race. Their heads were craned the other way. Sensing there was something amiss he backed off and was thus able to pick his way through the debris without undue delay.

No luck there, just uncanny attention to detail. He was more than a lap clear of Alberto Ascari (Ferrari 125) by the end (above).

BRITAIN'S BEST-SELLING SINGLES... WHEN FANGIO HAD HIS WITS ABOUT HIM
A bit difficult to ascertain, actually, because the *New Musical Express* did not come up with its pioneering chart concept until two years later. The Andrews Sisters and Perry Como were big news, however

May 26 2002
MONTE CARLO
STREET CIRCUIT
CIRCUIT LENGTH:
2.094miles / 3.370km

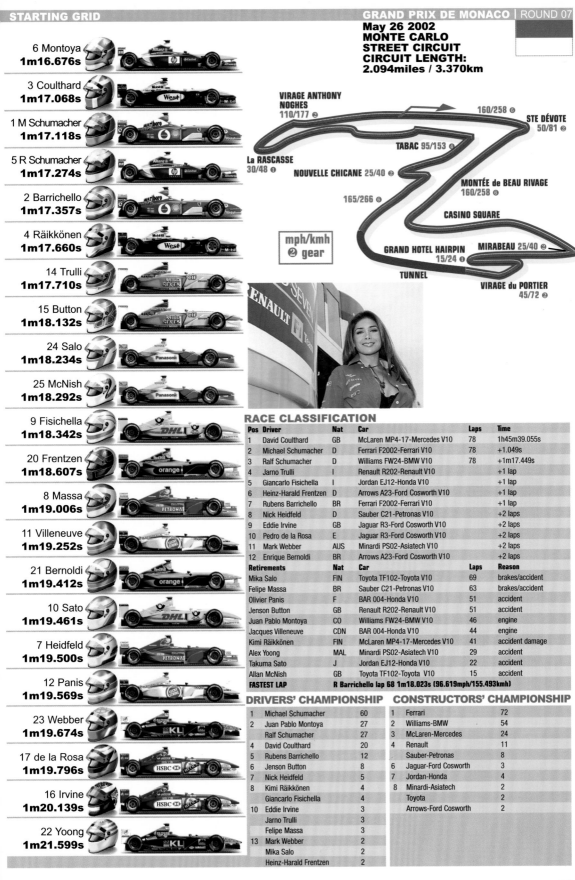

STARTING GRID

Pos	Driver	Time
6	Montoya	1m16.676s
3	Coulthard	1m17.068s
1	M Schumacher	1m17.118s
5	R Schumacher	1m17.274s
2	Barrichello	1m17.357s
4	Räikkönen	1m17.660s
14	Trulli	1m17.710s
15	Button	1m18.132s
24	Salo	1m18.234s
25	McNish	1m18.292s
9	Fisichella	1m18.342s
20	Frentzen	1m18.607s
8	Massa	1m19.006s
11	Villeneuve	1m19.252s
21	Bernoldi	1m19.412s
10	Sato	1m19.461s
7	Heidfeld	1m19.500s
12	Panis	1m19.569s
23	Webber	1m19.674s
17	de la Rosa	1m19.796s
16	Irvine	1m20.139s
22	Yoong	1m21.599s

Circuit markers:

VIRAGE ANTHONY NOGHES 110/177 ②
160/258 ⑥
STE DÉVOTE 50/81 ②
TABAC 95/153 ④
La RASCASSE 30/48 ①
NOUVELLE CHICANE 25/40 ②
MONTÉE de BEAU RIVAGE 160/258 ⑥
165/266 ⑥
CASINO SQUARE
GRAND HOTEL HAIRPIN 15/24 ①
MIRABEAU 25/40 ②
TUNNEL
VIRAGE du PORTIER 45/72 ②

mph/kmh
② gear

RACE CLASSIFICATION

Pos	Driver	Nat	Car	Laps	Time
1	David Coulthard	GB	McLaren MP4-17-Mercedes V10	78	1h45m39.055s
2	Michael Schumacher	D	Ferrari F2002-Ferrari V10	78	+1.049s
3	Ralf Schumacher	D	Williams FW24-BMW V10	78	+1m17.449s
4	Jarno Trulli	I	Renault R202-Renault V10		+1 lap
5	Giancarlo Fisichella	I	Jordan EJ12-Honda V10		+1 lap
6	Heinz-Harald Frentzen	D	Arrows A23-Ford Cosworth V10		+1 lap
7	Rubens Barrichello	BR	Ferrari F2002-Ferrari V10		+1 lap
8	Nick Heidfeld	D	Sauber C21-Petronas V10		+2 laps
9	Eddie Irvine	GB	Jaguar R3-Ford Cosworth V10		+2 laps
10	Pedro de la Rosa	E	Jaguar R3-Ford Cosworth V10		+2 laps
11	Mark Webber	AUS	Minardi PS02-Asiatech V10		+2 laps
12	Enrique Bernoldi	BR	Arrows A23-Ford Cosworth V10		+2 laps

Retirements	Nat	Car	Laps	Reason
Mika Salo	FIN	Toyota TF102-Toyota V10	69	brakes/accident
Felipe Massa	BR	Sauber C21-Petronas V10	63	brakes/accident
Olivier Panis	F	BAR 004-Honda V10	51	accident
Jenson Button	GB	Renault R202-Renault V10	51	accident
Juan Pablo Montoya	CO	Williams FW24-BMW V10	46	engine
Jacques Villeneuve	CDN	BAR 004-Honda V10	44	engine
Kimi Räikkönen	FIN	McLaren MP4-17-Mercedes V10	41	accident damage
Alex Yoong	MAL	Minardi PS02-Asiatech V10	29	accident
Takuma Sato	J	Jordan EJ12-Honda V10	22	accident
Allan McNish	GB	Toyota TF102-Toyota V10	15	accident

FASTEST LAP　　R Barrichello lap 68 1m18.023s (96.619mph/155.493kmh)

DRIVERS' CHAMPIONSHIP

	Driver	Pts
1	Michael Schumacher	60
2	Juan Pablo Montoya	27
	Ralf Schumacher	27
4	David Coulthard	20
5	Rubens Barrichello	12
6	Jenson Button	8
7	Nick Heidfeld	5
8	Kimi Räikkönen	4
	Giancarlo Fisichella	4
10	Eddie Irvine	3
	Jarno Trulli	3
	Felipe Massa	3
13	Mark Webber	2
	Mika Salo	2
	Heinz-Harald Frentzen	2

CONSTRUCTORS' CHAMPIONSHIP

	Constructor	Pts
1	Ferrari	72
2	Williams-BMW	54
3	McLaren-Mercedes	24
4	Renault	11
	Sauber-Petronas	8
6	Jaguar-Ford Cosworth	3
7	Jordan-Honda	4
8	Minardi-Asiatech	2
	Toyota	2
	Arrows-Ford Cosworth	2

GRAND PRIX AIR CANADA

IN 2001 MICHELIN AND WILLIAMS OVERTURNED
BRIDGESTONE AND FERRARI IN A STRAIGHTFORWARD
CANADIAN GP. THIS TIME THEY DIDN,T – AND IT WAS
FAR FROM SIMPLE

KING CRIMSON: "Have I won the world title yet?" The cricket
season might only just have been getting into its stride, but Schuey
was already more or less uncatchable (left). Hello clouds, hello sky...
Montoya bags his second straight retirement (above)

MICHAEL SCHUMACHER 70 POINTS, THE REST, WELL – WHO cares?

When we left Montreal the world champion had taken six from eight and everyone was talking about Michael wrapping it all up by July.

Formula One? Boring, isn't it? An entirely predictable non-event.

Except that it isn't. The problem, perhaps, is that the finer nuances of race strategy and performance tend to be the most influential aspects. Things like tyre performance, ambient temperature, the effect of fuel weight on lap times at any given circuit and teams' reactivity to changing circumstances. Hey, wake up you at the back!

If you're really paying attention, have done some background swotting up, bought five or six Sonys and subscribed to Bernie Ecclestone's digital TV, then you've got half a chance. The same chance as us, in fact. But if a) you've played a tough Sunday league game after a night on the razz and b) your roast lunch is still heavy on your beer gut, then sorry, but you're knackered, mate.

Take Montreal, for instance. Following hot on the heels of Monaco and David Coulthard's unexpected success, the casual observer might just have appreciated Michelin's tyre gamble and wondered what would happen here. But the real enthusiast would know that the Monte Carlo Michelin was a one-off and a tyre that soft wouldn't last two minutes in Montreal. So we should have been back to the status quo.

In so far as Michael won, we were. But that didn't explain why the two leading teams put their drivers on split strategies. Or why Ferrari did not call in the two-stopping Barrichello when the Safety Car

CANADA DRAY: McLaren wasn't especially competitive in Montreal, but Coulthard drove cannily to bag second (main shot); six appeal (below); overtaking alive and well in F1 shock (bottom) – Montoya passed Räikkönen and Ralf in one fell swoop

THE REAL ENTHUSIAST WOULD KNOW THAT THE MONTE CARLO MICHELIN WAS A ONE-OFF AND A TYRE THAT SOFT WOULDN'T LAST TWO MINUTES IN MONTREAL

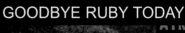

GOODBYE RUBY TODAY

emerged. Or why Williams' technical director Patrick Head thought Juan Pablo Montoya could have won had his BMW not expired.

Montoya started from pole position and led initially. Rubens Barrichello started behind Michael but got through Turn One in front of him and was quickly through into the lead because Montoya made a mistake out of the final chicane.

Michael ran third and lost a bit of ground to the first two early on, but was it enough to mean a different strategy? Almost certainly. If Michael is four seconds behind Rubens after five laps, it means only one thing.

And Ralf, the winner here a year ago? He was beaten away by Kimi Räikkönen and got stuck behind him. McLaren wasn't truly competitive here, so that was the end of Schuey Jnr's afternoon.

Rubens had gone for the softer Bridgestone, unlike Michael, and he was making a decent fist of his two-stopper until Jacques Villeneuve's BAR expired after just nine laps. It came to rest in an area where it could not be removed, hemmed in by concrete walls, but really wasn't in a dangerous position.

The FIA decided to take no chances and out came the Safety Car. Barrichello cursed. So much for maximising his two-stopper (see sidebar, right).

Montoya, also on a two-stopper, dived into the pits and rejoined still fifth. After three laps behind the Safety Car they were released again. Ralf had a go at Räikkönen and passed him into the final chicane, but they both made a hash of it. The younger Schuey was obliged to give the

IT'S ALL HYPOTHETICAL, WE KNOW, BUT INITIALLY the two-stopping Barrichello was running faster than the strategically like-minded Montoya.

The Safety Car (above) was not what the Brazilian wanted to see.

"I don't really understand why it was called out," Rubens said, "apart from the fact that it completely ruined my race."

As soon as Williams saw it, however, Montoya was immediately called in. The mechanics had not even left the garage when he entered the pit lane. Quicker to refuel under a caution period than not to. Had Ferrari done likewise, Rubens would still have been ahead of JPM on the road. So why the reluctance?

Well, Rubens would likely – not certainly – have exited behind Räikkönen and Schumacher Jnr and would have had to run behind them. They could not have foreseen the fortune/opportunism that allowed Montoya to nip straight past them both. Rubens would then have run longer than either and doubtless beaten them, but would he have beaten a two-stopping Montoya, who he already led on the road? Ferrari, remember, did not know that Montoya was coming in.

As it transpired, Montoya was within striking distance of Michael after his second stop and Rubens would have been a little closer still, in the same car on softer, blister-free Bridgestones.

Perhaps Ferrari didn't want that. As Ross Brawn pointed out after Austria, there are more clandestine ways to orchestrate the final result.

"It was a close call with Rubens and the Safety Car and I'm not entirely happy I got it right," Brawn admitted afterwards.

More likely though, these things have to be called in the blink of an eye and the ramifications of the Safety Car for Michael were probably first priority to be crunched through the computer.

SCOT LAD THE BRAVE:
Coulthard fends off Barrichello (above), despite being armed only with a Mercedes V10. Right, fire-resistant overalls are not strictly necessary in the paddock, ladies

MICHAEL HAD A POTENTIAL PROBLEM. RÄIKKÖNEN AND RALF WERE CLOSER TO HIM THAN THEY SHOULD HAVE BEEN. HE COULD GET TRAPPED BEHIND THEM LONG ENOUGH TO BRING MONTOYA BACK INTO PLAY

place back and Montoya brilliantly jumped them both into Turn One.

It was now Rubens, Michael, Juan Pablo. The Brazilian made his first stop on lap 26 and that left Michael leading Juan Pablo and, on lighter fuel, going away.

Michael though, had a potential problem. The Safety Car period meant that Räikkönen and Ralf were closer to him than they would ordinarily have been. The McLaren, almost certainly, would run a long stint and a one-stopping Michael could get trapped behind him long enough to bring Montoya back into play.

Michael stopped on lap 38 of 70 and allowed the Williams to lead. The Ferrari got out just ahead of Räikkönen, who ran for another seven laps. Michael was now fuel-heavy and Montoya continued to open out his lead to almost 13s before stopping for the final time on lap 51. He rejoined 8.5s behind the lead Ferrari with 18 to go.

The simple fact is that Montoya's BMW let go after another four laps, by which time he had closed on Michael and forced the Ferrari to respond.

Williams thought Michael was in trouble with fuel, because he'd made a quick stop to stay ahead of Räikkönen, and that his tyres were badly blistered. In the end he didn't have to hurry. Could he have done? "No problem," the champion said, with a grin. Williams was not convinced.

FLASHBACK
September 23 1973, Mosport Park, Canada

SLICK USE OF THE SAFETY CAR IN MODERN Formula One is something we have come to take for granted. Incident occurs. Silver Mercedes-Benz is deployed. Field bunches up. Ferrari makes canny tactical pit stop. Track is cleared. Race resumes. Ferrari wins. But it wasn't always thus.

Conditions were miserable when the 1973 Canadian GP began. Pole position winner Ronnie Peterson (Lotus 72) led initially, but Niki Lauda (BRM P160E) made a flying start from eighth on the grid and, somewhat improbably, soon worked his way into the lead. He stayed there until stopping to fit intermediate tyres on the drying track. Wrong call: slicks were the way to go.

The complexion of the race changed dramatically on lap 33 of 80, when Jody Scheckter (McLaren M23) and François Cevert (Tyrrell 006) collided. For the first time in F1 history, out came what was then known as the Pace Car. This was supposed to run ahead of the leader – Lauda's team-mate Jean-Pierre Beltoise according to the official lap chart, although the flurry of tyre stops created an air of confusion and some thought Jackie Oliver (Shadow DN1) was in front. Either way, the officials picked up Howden Ganley's Iso Marlboro. This was running better than usual, but certainly wasn't leading.

The cock-up allowed Peter Revson (McLaren M23), Beltoise and Oliver to gain almost a lap on their closest rivals – most notably Emerson Fittipaldi (Lotus 72). The Brazilian drove a stormer once the race resumed and Lotus thought its man had won, but amid pandemonium Revson was directed to the top step of the podium, ahead of Fittipaldi and Oliver. It was probably the right call, although even McLaren wasn't sure because its own lap chart had gone horribly wrong...

BRITAIN'S BEST-SELLING SINGLES... WHEN CANADA COULD HAVE DONE WITH TRANSPONDER TECHNOLOGY

1 WIZZARD	Angel Fingers
2 DONNY OSMOND	Young Love
3 DAVID ESSEX	Rock On
4 BARRY BLUE	Dancing On A Saturday Night
5 AL MARTINO	Spanish Eyes

June 9 2002
CIRCUIT GILLES
VILLENEUVE,
ILE NOTRE DAME,
MONTREAL
CIRCUIT LENGTH: 2.710miles / 4.361km

6 Montoya
1m 12.836s

1 M Schumacher
1m 13.018s

2 Barrichello
1m 13.280s

5 R Schumacher
1m 13.301s

4 Räikkönen
1m 13.898s

9 Fisichella
1m 14.132s

7 Heidfeld
1m 14.139s

3 Coulthard
1m 14.385s

11 Villeneuve
1m 14.564s

14 Trulli
1m 14.688s

12 Panis
1m 14.713s

8 Massa
1m 14.823s

15 Button
1m 14.854s

16 Irvine
1m 14.882s

10 Sato
1m 14.940s

17 de la Rosa
1m 15.089s

21 Bernoldi
1m 15.102s

24 Salo
1m 15.111s

20 Frentzen
1m 15.115s

25 McNish
1m 15.321s

23 Webber
1m 15.508s

22 Yoong
1m 17.347s

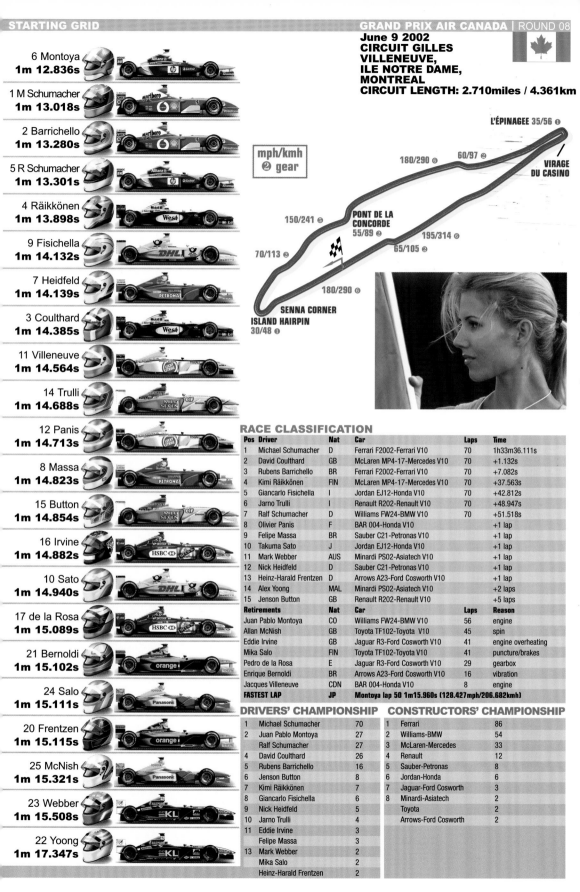

L'ÉPINAGEE 35/56 ❶

180/290 ❻   60/97 ❷

VIRAGE
DU CASINO

mph/kmh
❷ gear

150/241 ❺

PONT DE LA
CONCORDE
55/89 ❷

195/314 ❻

70/113 ❷   65/105 ❷

180/290 ❻

SENNA CORNER
ISLAND HAIRPIN
30/48 ❶

RACE CLASSIFICATION

Pos	Driver	Nat	Car	Laps	Time
1	Michael Schumacher	D	Ferrari F2002-Ferrari V10	70	1h33m36.111s
2	David Coulthard	GB	McLaren MP4-17-Mercedes V10	70	+1.132s
3	Rubens Barrichello	BR	Ferrari F2002-Ferrari V10	70	+7.082s
4	Kimi Räikkönen	FIN	McLaren MP4-17-Mercedes V10	70	+37.563s
5	Giancarlo Fisichella	I	Jordan EJ12-Honda V10	70	+42.812s
6	Jarno Trulli	I	Renault R202-Renault V10	70	+48.947s
7	Ralf Schumacher	D	Williams FW24-BMW V10	70	+51.518s
8	Olivier Panis	F	BAR 004-Honda V10		+1 lap
9	Felipe Massa	BR	Sauber C21-Petronas V10		+1 lap
10	Takuma Sato	J	Jordan EJ12-Honda V10		+1 lap
11	Mark Webber	AUS	Minardi PS02-Asiatech V10		+1 lap
12	Nick Heidfeld	D	Sauber C21-Petronas V10		+1 lap
13	Heinz-Harald Frentzen	D	Arrows A23-Ford Cosworth V10		+1 lap
14	Alex Yoong	MAL	Minardi PS02-Asiatech V10		+2 laps
15	Jenson Button	GB	Renault R202-Renault V10		+5 laps

Retirements	Nat	Car	Laps	Reason
Juan Pablo Montoya	CO	Williams FW24-BMW V10	56	engine
Allan McNish	GB	Toyota TF102-Toyota V10	45	spin
Eddie Irvine	GB	Jaguar R3-Ford Cosworth V10	41	engine overheating
Mika Salo	FIN	Toyota TF102-Toyota V10	41	puncture/brakes
Pedro de la Rosa	E	Jaguar R3-Ford Cosworth V10	29	gearbox
Enrique Bernoldi	BR	Arrows A23-Ford Cosworth V10	16	vibration
Jacques Villeneuve	CDN	BAR 004-Honda V10	8	engine
FASTEST LAP	**JP**	**Montoya lap 50 1m15.960s (128.427mph/206.682kmh)**		

DRIVERS' CHAMPIONSHIP

1	Michael Schumacher	70
2	Juan Pablo Montoya	27
	Ralf Schumacher	27
4	David Coulthard	26
5	Rubens Barrichello	16
6	Jenson Button	8
7	Kimi Räikkönen	7
8	Giancarlo Fisichella	6
9	Nick Heidfeld	5
10	Jarno Trulli	4
11	Eddie Irvine	3
	Felipe Massa	3
13	Mark Webber	2
	Mika Salo	2
	Heinz-Harald Frentzen	2

CONSTRUCTORS' CHAMPIONSHIP

1	Ferrari	86
2	Williams-BMW	54
3	McLaren-Mercedes	33
4	Renault	12
5	Sauber-Petronas	8
6	Jordan-Honda	6
7	Jaguar-Ford Cosworth	3
8	Minardi-Asiatech	2
	Toyota	2
	Arrows-Ford Cosworth	2

ALLIANZ GRAND PRIX OF EUROPE

WILLIAMS LOCKED OUT THE FRONT ROW
ON SATURDAY, BUT A DIFFERENT STRAIN
OF DOMINANCE WAS APPARENT 24 HOURS
LATER. SIMPLY RED? TAKE IT AS READ

MESSAGE IN A BATTLE: "Oi! You two. What
d'you think you're doing? Stop racing. Now."
Barrichello and Schuey hold station (right).
Left, how come Rubens can't afford razor blades
on his salary?

RUBENS WAS A SECOND CLEAR AS THEY FLASHED ACROSS THE LINE. IT WAS THE BEST OPENING LAP ANYBODY COULD REMEMBER FOR A LONG TIME

THE AUSTRIAN FURORE WAS SIX WEEKS REMOVED.

Ferrari was up before the FIA World Council three days hence. But here, at the revised Nürburgring, Rubens led Michael after the second scheduled round of stops. What would the team do?

Ferrari could be damned either way. If it told Rubens to let Michael past again, who knows what the reaction might have been. It's hard to imagine the Germans booing their own man at home.

Then again, if they told the pair to maintain station, they were arguably manipulating the result again.

In the end option two prevailed and Barrichello finally took an overdue second career win. A fabulous opening lap was the key but you still felt that maybe Rubens should have had Austria and Michael this one.

Michael was magnanimous afterwards: "We were free to race until after the second pit stops," he confirmed. "Rubens drove superbly, without any mistakes, and I didn't. So he deserved to win."

The Ferraris lined up behind a blue-and-white Williams wall for the first race at a heavily reworked Nürburgring, where the first-corner Esses had been bulldozed to make way for a tight new complex that added 600 metres to the lap.

WILLIAMS' TELLING OVERTURE: pained expressions from BMW racing bosses Mario Theissen and Gerhard Berger (with Sir Frank, inset top) as they realise their blokes are already in trouble (main shot). And it's only lap one... Michael in mistake shocker (inset, below). Montoya heads the McLarens (above) before taking one of them out

LAST ORDERS, GENTS?

IF FERRARI REALLY HAD NO QUALMS ABOUT what it did in Austria, why didn't the team order Rubens to give way at the Nürburgring too?

"In Austria we were not arrogant enough to think we were going to win the championship," Schumacher said. "I'm not saying that we are arrogant enough to say that now. But that was race six and this is race nine. Our position is more comfortable. I think that justifies the situation."

He was certainly right about one thing. Their position was indeed comfortable. Michelin opted for soft compounds again in Germany and went a bit too far. The Williams men were in big trouble trying to make a set last until half-distance.

"Our tyres gave extremely high performance," said Michelin's motorsport director Pierre Dupasquier, "but it is clear that trying to run a one-stop race strategy was marginal."

So why did Williams and McLaren try?

On the harder primary tyre or the softer option, there was a performance drop-off that could be limited by scrubbing the rubber beforehand. But there was insufficient time to scrub enough tyres to run a two-stop race.

Of the two McLaren was in better shape and David Coulthard was crawling all over Montoya. At the start of lap 28 DC got a decent exit from the last corner and towed the Williams down the straight.

"He went to protect the inside of Turn One and then moved me across to the outside," Coulthard said. "I gave him the room on the inside so that we could do the corner together and my plan was to be on the inside for the next one. But he lost the back end, went into the side of my car and that was it." There was sarcastic applause from the Scot as he climbed out.

Jenson Button's Michelin-shod Renault also managed to lap faster and Williams' chief operations engineer Sam Michael said: "It's clear where our problem lies. We need to make the chassis work on a softer tyre. It's our problem, not Michelin's."

As the lights faded Montoya chopped smartly across from his third consecutive pole to protect the inside line. Schumacher Jnr drew alongside to his left and pinched him tight going in. So tight, in fact, that they touched and the Colombian suffered a bent steering arm.

Ralf pushed the issue so hard because he wanted to make the most of his fresh rear tyres, but Montoya wasn't impressed. The private Williams tussle allowed Barrichello to oust the Colombian at Turn Two and he knifed inside Ralf at the Dunlop Kurve. Rubens was a second clear as they flashed across the line. It was the best opening lap anybody could remember for a long time.

Fair enough, as things transpired the Ferraris were on a two-stop strategy while Williams and McLaren had gone for one, so Rubens was lighter, but it was still a fine effort. And a race-winning one. Michael, who blasted past Montoya into the Veedol Chicane, was already three seconds behind by the end of lap one.

Michael was soon on his brother's gearbox and displaced him up the inside of the RTL Kurve on lap three, by which time Rubens was 3.5s to the good.

With 10 of the 60 laps down, Schumacher had all but wiped out his

JORDAN WANDER: four of these drivers have got the right idea, Giancarlo Fisichella hasn't. Worse, he'd just clattered out-of-shot team-mate Sato, too

MICHAEL EVEN HAD TIME TO SPIN AND STILL GET OUT AHEAD OF RALF. BUT AS FAR AS WINNING THE RACE WAS CONCERNED IT WAS A COSTLY ERROR

team-mate's early advantage and it was obvious that nobody was going to get near Ferrari. A soft Michelin might have enabled Williams to take pole but Bridgestone had the better race tyre. Ralf Schumacher was 18 seconds behind already and the Ferraris were going to be able to stop without losing their lead.

Michael, in fact, even had time to indulge in a spin in Turn 10 and still get out ahead of Ralf. But as far as winning the race was concerned it was a costly error.

"I don't know exactly what happened," he said. "There might have been some oil or dirt, because Rubens said later that he had a problem there as well, but I guess I got too close. I was pushing hard because I knew we were due to stop and that he was staying out one lap longer. I still hoped to be able to jump ahead of him."

His rare mistake meant that by the time they both had new Bridgestones and were back up to speed, Rubens was 8.3s clear. Michael proved that without the mistake he would almost certainly have taken the lead, because his first lap on new rubber was a 1:32.226s – the fastest of the race by more than half a second.

With the final stops approaching Michael had taken 6s out of Rubens and was just 2.5s behind. The world champion blasted in on lap 43. There was precious little to choose between new tyres/heavier fuel and used Bridgestones/light fuel. As soon as he was back on the track Michael set a new fastest time in sector two. Rubens responded with personal bests in sectors one and two as he stayed out two laps more. Then Michael lost a bit of time as he caught the battle for sixth, between the Saubers and Jarno Trulli. Rubens was still 2s to the good as he pitted two laps later and shot back out. Out went the order to maintain station. Job done. Nobody else stood a chance.

FLASHBACK

October 6 1985, Brands Hatch, England

FOR DECADES THE GRAND PRIX OF EUROPE WAS an honorary title bestowed intermittently on race promoters. In 1983, however, it became a stand-alone world championship event.

Although it has since attained apparently permanent calendar status, it was initially an occasional wheeze to allow selected countries a second annual grand prix. Brands Hatch was the first host.

Two years later the GP of Europe returned to Kent, where Nigel Mansell was at the centre of a media feeding-frenzy. The Englishman was coming towards the end of his first season with Williams-Honda, the promise of which had yet to yield any victories.

He qualified third but was beaten off the line by neighbouring team-mate Keke Rosberg and slotted into fourth place. On lap seven Rosberg tried to wrest the lead from Ayrton Senna (Lotus 97T) at Surtees and spun. The following Nelson Piquet (Brabham BT54) hit the errant Finn and Mansell slipped into second. Rosberg continued with a puncture and pitted for fresh tyres. He rejoined almost a lap down – just ahead of Senna, whom Mansell was challenging with increasing vigour.

Lap nine. Senna is right on Rosberg's tail. The Finn impedes him. It's slight and subtle, but enough to check the Brazilian's momentum. Mansell pounces. The crowd goes mad.

Mansell had led races before but always managed to stumble. Not today, though. At the 72nd attempt he finally won a GP (above). True, Scottish legend Jim Clark only entered that many and won 25 times, but it was a start. Alain Prost (McLaren-TAG) finished fourth, more than a minute behind, to clinch his first world title, but that wasn't why fans invaded the track. Mansellmania was born.

BRITAIN'S BEST-SELLING SINGLES... WHEN NIGEL MANSELL'S F1 CAREER FINALLY TOOK OFF	
1 JENNIFER RUSH	The Power Of Love
2 MIDGE URE	If I Was
3 COLONEL ABRAMS	Trapped
4 RED BOX	Lean On Me
5 BILLY IDOL	Rebel Yell

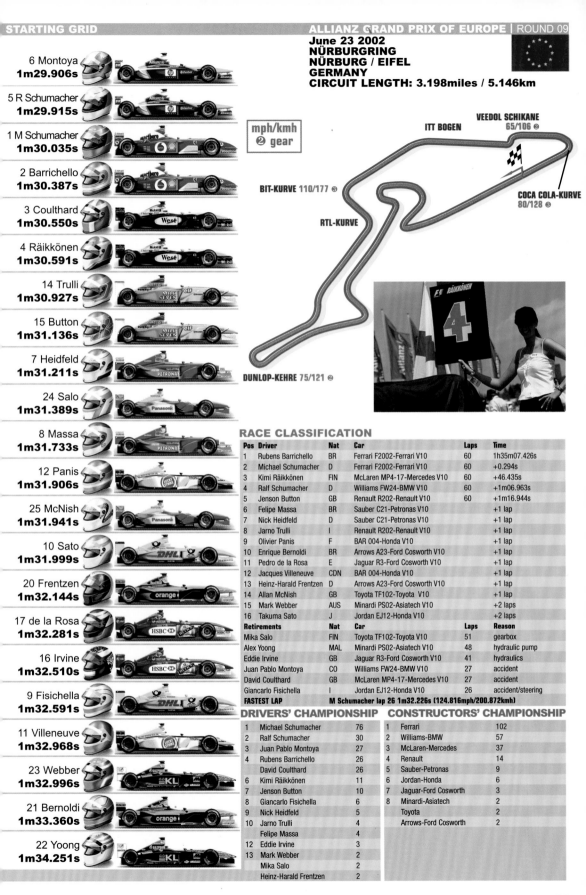

Starting Grid

Pos	Driver	Time
6	Montoya	1m29.906s
5	R Schumacher	1m29.915s
1	M Schumacher	1m30.035s
2	Barrichello	1m30.387s
3	Coulthard	1m30.550s
4	Räikkönen	1m30.591s
14	Trulli	1m30.927s
15	Button	1m31.136s
7	Heidfeld	1m31.211s
24	Salo	1m31.389s
8	Massa	1m31.733s
12	Panis	1m31.906s
25	McNish	1m31.941s
10	Sato	1m31.999s
20	Frentzen	1m32.144s
17	de la Rosa	1m32.281s
16	Irvine	1m32.510s
9	Fisichella	1m32.591s
11	Villeneuve	1m32.968s
23	Webber	1m32.996s
21	Bernoldi	1m33.360s
22	Yoong	1m34.251s

June 23 2002
NÜRBURGRING
NÜRBURG / EIFEL
GERMANY
CIRCUIT LENGTH: 3.198miles / 5.146km

mph/kmh
❷ gear

VEEDOL SCHIKANE 65/106 ❷
ITT BOGEN
BIT-KURVE 110/177 ❸
COCA COLA-KURVE 80/128 ❸
RTL-KURVE
DUNLOP-KEHRE 75/121 ❷

RACE CLASSIFICATION

Pos	Driver	Nat	Car	Laps	Time
1	Rubens Barrichello	BR	Ferrari F2002-Ferrari V10	60	1h35m07.426s
2	Michael Schumacher	D	Ferrari F2002-Ferrari V10	60	+0.294s
3	Kimi Räikkönen	FIN	McLaren MP4-17-Mercedes V10	60	+46.435s
4	Ralf Schumacher	D	Williams FW24-BMW V10	60	+1m06.963s
5	Jenson Button	GB	Renault R202-Renault V10	60	+1m16.944s
6	Felipe Massa	BR	Sauber C21-Petronas V10		+1 lap
7	Nick Heidfeld	D	Sauber C21-Petronas V10		+1 lap
8	Jarno Trulli	I	Renault R202-Renault V10		+1 lap
9	Olivier Panis	F	BAR 004-Honda V10		+1 lap
10	Enrique Bernoldi	BR	Arrows A23-Ford Cosworth V10		+1 lap
11	Pedro de la Rosa	E	Jaguar R3-Ford Cosworth V10		+1 lap
12	Jacques Villeneuve	CDN	BAR 004-Honda V10		+1 lap
13	Heinz-Harald Frentzen	D	Arrows A23-Ford Cosworth V10		+1 lap
14	Allan McNish	GB	Toyota TF102-Toyota V10		+1 lap
15	Mark Webber	AUS	Minardi PS02-Asiatech V10		+2 laps
16	Takuma Sato	J	Jordan EJ12-Honda V10		+2 laps

Retirements	Nat	Car	Laps	Reason
Mika Salo	FIN	Toyota TF102-Toyota V10	51	gearbox
Alex Yoong	MAL	Minardi PS02-Asiatech V10	48	hydraulic pump
Eddie Irvine	GB	Jaguar R3-Ford Cosworth V10	41	hydraulics
Juan Pablo Montoya	CO	Williams FW24-BMW V10	27	accident
David Coulthard	GB	McLaren MP4-17-Mercedes V10	27	accident
Giancarlo Fisichella	I	Jordan EJ12-Honda V10	26	accident/steering

FASTEST LAP M Schumacher lap 26 1m32.226s (124.816mph/200.872kmh)

DRIVERS' CHAMPIONSHIP

1	Michael Schumacher	76
2	Ralf Schumacher	30
3	Juan Pablo Montoya	27
4	Rubens Barrichello	26
	David Coulthard	26
6	Kimi Räikkönen	11
7	Jenson Button	10
8	Giancarlo Fisichella	6
9	Nick Heidfeld	5
10	Jarno Trulli	4
	Felipe Massa	4
12	Eddie Irvine	3
13	Mark Webber	2
	Mika Salo	2
	Heinz-Harald Frentzen	2

CONSTRUCTORS' CHAMPIONSHIP

1	Ferrari	102
2	Williams-BMW	57
3	McLaren-Mercedes	37
4	Renault	14
5	Sauber-Petronas	9
6	Jordan-Honda	6
7	Jaguar-Ford Cosworth	3
8	Minardi-Asiatech	2
	Toyota	2
	Arrows-Ford Cosworth	2

SOFA SO GOOD

AFTER MORE THAN 50 YEARS IN THE COMMENTARY BOOTH, MURRAY WALKER COULD HAVE BEEN FORGIVEN FOR PUTTING HIS FEET UP DURING HIS FIRST YEAR OF RETIREMENT. AND SO HE DID... BUT USUALLY ONLY WHEN SETTLING DOWN TO WATCH A FORMULA ONE RACE FROM THE COMFORT OF HIS LIVING ROOM

SOME RETIREMENT, THIS. MURRAY WALKER, official voice of British motor racing, might not have been a permanent fixture at grands prix in 2002, but he watched all of them live in one way or another.

Did he miss his old job? He ponders, then grins and says. "I feel completely at peace about not being at the races because it was my decision to stop. I had been doing the job for 52 years and wanted to get out with dignity, while I was still reasonably close to the top. Would I have liked to continue? Definitely. Would I still have been able to do the job? Of course. But it is always better to stop too soon than too late. As a result, I certainly haven't been sitting at home feeling bitter and twisted because I'm not doing it any more.

"The thing I missed most was probably the travel, because I have always enjoyed globetrotting. That plus the buzz and the gossip. It is amazing how quickly you lose touch with some things, whereas when I was a permanent part of the paddock bits of information sort of passed on by osmosis.

"I enjoyed myself immensely at the races I attended in 2002 and didn't realise quite how many friends I had until I saw them all again, which was wonderful. I love F1 but really wouldn't want to go to all the events now. I enjoyed it when I had a job to do but I don't want to hang around like a spare part. It's OK to do that occasionally, but not all the time."

The first race of the season in Melbourne was broadcast live at an anti-social hour for British TV viewers. The temptation to programme the video might have been overwhelming for the majority, but Murray was up and about at four in the morning to compere a reception at a

Renault showroom in west London. "I was hosting a big party for the opening grand prix," he says. "I interviewed Renault F1 boss Flavio Briatore and Jenson Button live from the grid, via a satellite link, then watched events unfold and shouted at the screen a bit for the benefit of guests."

When he's not wired for sound, however, grands prix in the Walker household are peaceful. "Contrary to what you might expect," he says, "I sit calmly and dispassionately and make copious notes, because I remain very interested and still have a number of professional commitments to fulfil. But I don't jump up and down or shout at the screen. All that emotion used to come about because I was communicating and that was my way of doing it."

And would he have been able to summon a full-on laryngeal assault in 2002 given the repetitive nature of many races? Almost certainly.

"I have found it very absorbing to see Ferrari reaping the rewards of all the effort it has put in during recent years," he says. "I can understand how this year's results might have put off some casual viewers, but I think the team deserves everything that has come its way."

In his first season since handing over the microphone he attended only two F1 races – Silverstone and Indianapolis – but filled spare time in-between by writing and promoting a book (via a world tour), compiling a video, doing some feature slots for ITV and maintaining his regular, twice-per-week gym sessions. He didn't have to do quite so much travel as before, but it was still the kind of schedule that might tax a 30-year-old.

Murray turned 79 in October – but he still has plenty to do and just as much to offer.

FIVE MURRAY WALKER FACTS

1 He made his first British GP commentary in 1949, sitting in a wooden shack on the outside of Stowe Corner at Silverstone

2 He undertook his first full F1 season with the BBC in 1978 and his last with ITV in 2001

3 During his days in the advertising industry he was responsible for alerting the British public to the fact that, "Trill makes budgies bounce with health"

4 He once came within an ace of thumping James Hunt during a live broadcast, when the late world champion snatched away his microphone

5 For 2003, the second season of his retirement, he has so far pencilled the Australian, Monaco and British GPs into his live events diary

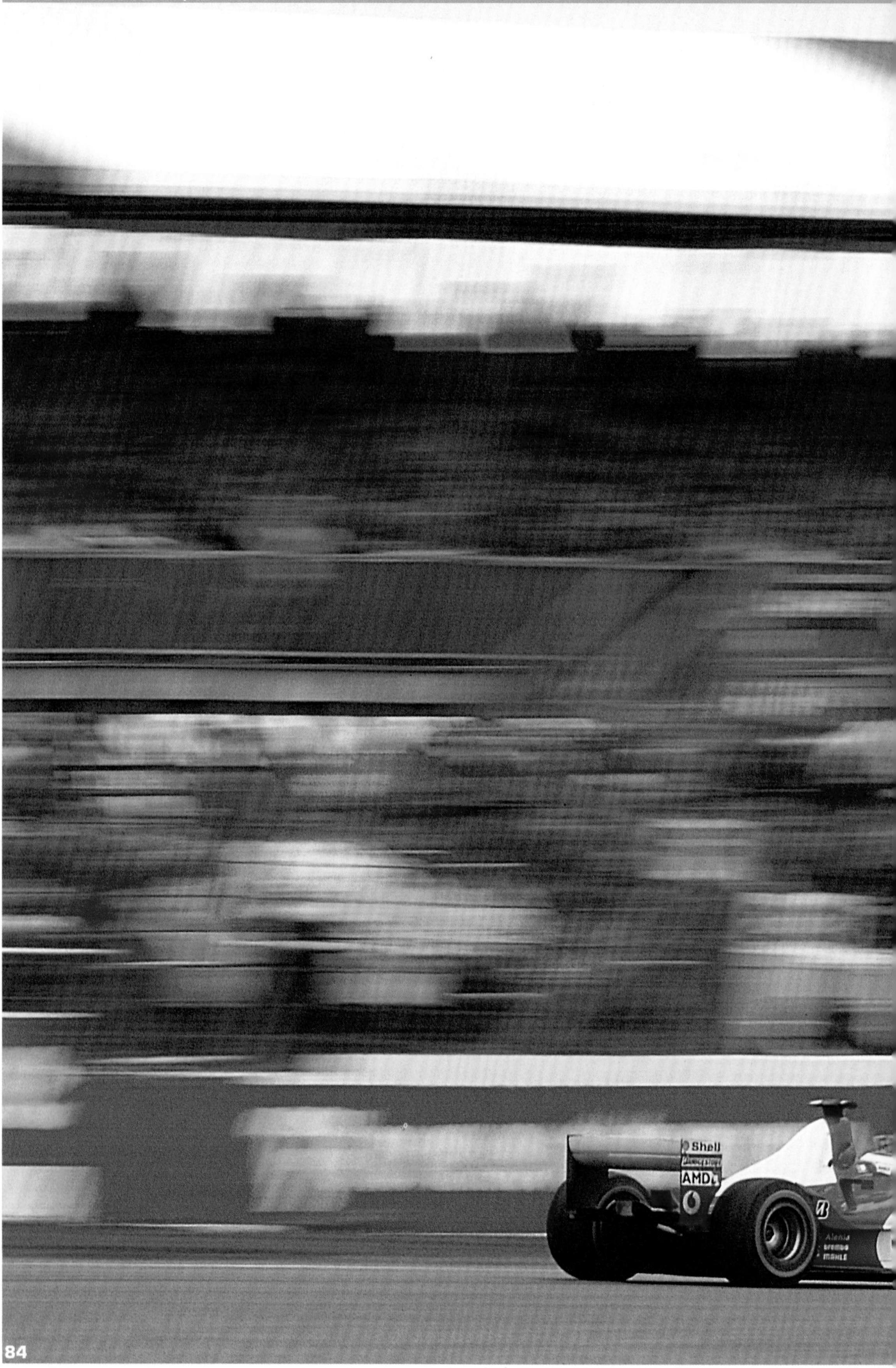
Shell
AMD

FOSTER'S BRITISH GRAND PRIX

MONTOYA HAD TO BE AT HIS INSPIRED BEST TO
NICK POLE POSITION, BUT THEN IT RAINED SO WE
WERE CONDEMNED TO FIND YET ANOTHER
PHOTO OF SCHUEY

TORTOISE AND THE HARE Montoya's fourth straight pole position
yielded, er, a fourth straight defeat. Schuey cruised home (above)
and Juan Pablo eventually had to concede to Rubens, too (left)

THE ARRIVAL OF RAIN SIMPLIFIED THINGS CONSIDERABLY FOR MICHAEL. MONTOYA EKED OUT A FEW SECONDS AS THEY SKATED AROUND ON THEIR DRIES, BUT AS SOON AS THEY HAD SWITCHED TO WETS IT WAS NO CONTEST

THE BRITISH GRAND PRIX WAS AN EXERCISE IN FRUSTRATION

for anyone without access to a set of Bridgestone intermediates. Chief among them was Juan Pablo Montoya, who claimed a superb pole position for Williams.

There had been little indication that Montoya had such a lap in him. Rubens Barrichello looked likely to provide Michael Schumacher's chief opposition as Juan tried to dial out understeer. Then, suddenly, bang! There was only 0.03s between Juan and Rubens, who ousted Schumacher by even less, but down at Williams they were deeply impressed.

"It was a very special lap," technical director Patrick Head confirmed. "We thought the same about his Monaco pole because ours is a big, long car and we hadn't been great there recently, but this was on a par." Gerhard Berger liked it too. "It was just a very big balls lap," he said, with a grin.

Michael started his weekend in uncharacteristic fashion by spinning first time through a damp Abbey early on Friday morning. A little sheepish, he watched the rest of the session from a deckchair under a marshal's umbrella, for which he traded his driving gloves. That was a

DOCUMENTARY, MY DEAR WATSON

BIG IN JAPAN: Takuma Sato's presence in F1 (above) sent TV figures soaring in his homeland, even though his debut season beset by problems. Engine failure put him out at Silverstone. Below right, Frentzen tracks down Fisichella. Below left, Heidfeld took sixth. Below without any cotton north of their shorts, two more girls in the pits without a pass

good deal for the official. The post remained deserted for the rest of the day as the chap dashed off to Sotheby's...

Come the qualifying hour Michael was not pleased to be only third quickest, but he didn't need to concern himself unduly about Rubens on Sunday. An electronic glitch caused the Brazilian to stall before the final formation lap and he had to start from the back.

In the dry opening stages Michael sat behind Montoya and looked menacing. He thought about trying to pass on a couple of occasions but Juan Pablo, going deep into the braking areas, was not about to be intimidated.

The arrival of rain simplified things considerably for Michael. Montoya eked out a few seconds as they skated around on their dries, but as soon as they had switched to wets it was no contest. The Bridgestone runners went for intermediates while the Michelin teams, knowing their intermediate was off the pace, took wets.

Montoya could only laugh as Schumacher drove around his Williams as if it wasn't there on the way out of Abbey for the 16th time. Barrichello, fifth after his stop, made short work of Coulthard, ate up Jarno Trulli and Montoya and put the Ferraris first and second after 19

WHEN THE RAIN CAME, KIMI RÄIKKÖNEN'S arrival in the pit lane was clearly a surprise to McLaren, which had no tyres ready for him. David Coulthard, meanwhile, radioed his intention to come in, received no confirmation and had to stay out.

"There was a discussion," explained McLaren MD Martin Whitmarsh, "and it was agreed that Kimi was staying out, but he came in. So whether he communicated and none of us heard, I don't know."

In fairness, it was a bit more complicated than that, as team principal Ron Dennis pointed out.

"One of the digital TV soundtracks was filtering through to our pit radio," he said, "so we had commentators in the background throughout most of the race. Kimi stopped without any instruction and David did the same thing two laps later. We were struggling with communication all the way through. It wasn't the only reason for our problems but it was extremely disruptive and certainly didn't help..."

The McLaren management on the pit wall couldn't hear their drivers whenever one of the digital commentators said anything. The mechanics (above) could hear, but given that they take their cues from the pit wall it wasn't a lot of help. It must have been particularly galling for them when former McLaren racer John Watson told Sky viewers that people pay to see this sort of thing at a pantomime, not a grand prix.

McLaren gambled and Coulthard took on dry tyres when he made his second stop. Sod's law said that it rained again... He was back five laps later, this time for Michelin's shallow wet. Result? No grip and a spin coming out of Bridge.

Whitmarsh reckoned it was the team's worst race since the 1995 GP of Europe, when its drivers had struggled to keep Jean-Denis Delétraz's unfancied Pacific at bay.

MAKE MINE A POINT: Panis, BAR boss David Richards and Villeneuve had something to smile about after the team notched its first top-six finishes of the campaign

NICK HEIDFELD'S AFTERNOON TOLD YOU EVERYTHING YOU NEED TO KNOW ABOUT THE ADAPTABILITY OF THE BRIDGESTONE INTERMEDIATE

laps. It would be another 25 before the circuit dried out.

In the meantime, the Bridgestones were anything between two and four seconds a lap quicker than the Michelin cars, depending on who was pedalling.

Here was a gilt-edged opportunity for Arrows. Okay, Montoya was out of reach, but a fuel rig malfunction forced Ralf Schumacher to pit again, so he was out of contention, and the McLarens were having a complete nightmare (see Page 87).

Heinz-Harald Frentzen is superb on a wet track and had just knifed past Jacques Villeneuve's similarly Bridgestone-shod BAR to take fourth place when he was cruelly robbed by an engine failure. Arrows felt the blow even more keenly this particular weekend because financial issues were clouding the team's future. It had been forced to skip Friday's free practice sessions altogether.

Villeneuve was competitive in the wet on Friday and happy to discover that the BAR still had top-10 potential in the dry qualifying hour.

Thanks to the use of weather spotters in local villages, plus team principal David Richards' helicopter pilot flying upwind to provide the very latest information, BAR's pit stops were superbly timed and the team's first points of the campaign arrived in a double helping. Villeneuve took fourth and team-mate Olivier Panis enjoyed some long-overdue good fortune to follow Jacques across the line.

The result was not without sacrifice. Chief mechanic Alastair Gibson had left his wife in labour to carry out his track duties, although he was off to the hospital at the double as soon as the flag fell.

Nick Heidfeld claimed the final point for Sauber and his afternoon told you everything you need to know about the adaptability of the Bridgestone intermediate. At his mid race stop, with the track drying, Heidfeld bolted on another set of inters because the clouds were threatening again. The rain didn't materialise but the tyres got him through to the end for a point. Impressive, that.

FLASHBACK

July 19 1975, Silverstone, England

THINGS HAD CHANGED SINCE SILVERSTONE LAST hosted the British GP, two years earlier.

On that occasion the race was marked by a colossal accident at the end of the first lap, when McLaren's raw rookie Jody Scheckter lost control through the ultra-fast right-hand sweep at Woodcote and triggered a chain-reaction pile-up.

That spelt the death knell for one of the sport's greatest corners. In its place? A quick, but less spectacular, chicane.

This time the race started quietly enough, with Carlos Pace (Brabham BT44B) getting ahead of pole position winner Tom Pryce (Shadow DN5). Before 20 laps were run, however, it began to drizzle. Some drivers pitted for wets, others pressed on with slicks, which looked to be the correct choice as the track soon dried once more.

Then, as the race drew towards a close, the rain returned – and this time it was a torrent. No one had time to get back to the pits. Jean-Pierre Jarier (Shadow DN5) started the ball rolling by crashing at Woodcote on lap 55. On the next lap three drivers went off the road at Stowe and eight more at Club. Out came the red flag and Emerson Fittipaldi (McLaren M23) teetered across the line to claim victory.

Results were taken after 55 laps: Pace, Jody Scheckter (Tyrrell 007), James Hunt (Hesketh 308) and Mark Donohue (March 751) were classified second to fifth, even though their cars were steaming in the scrapyard that had built up on the south side of the circuit (above).

Curiously, professional crasher Vittorio Brambilla (March 751) didn't hit anything and, Fittipaldi apart, was the only member of the top six whose car was still in one piece by the end.

July 7 2002
SILVERSTONE GRAND PRIX CIRCUIT, TOWCESTER, NORTHAMPTONSHIRE
CIRCUIT LENGTH: 3.194miles / 5.141km

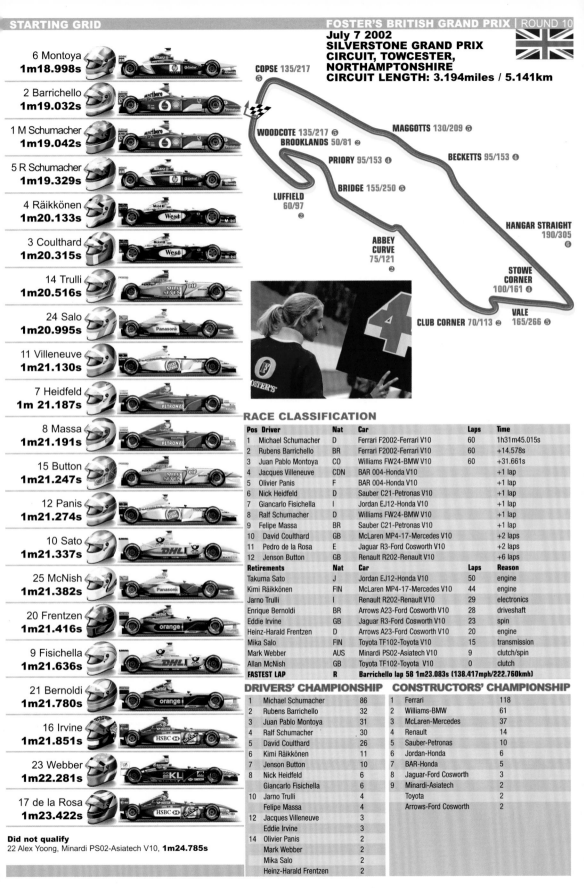

6 Montoya	**1m18.998s**
2 Barrichello	**1m19.032s**
1 M Schumacher	**1m19.042s**
5 R Schumacher	**1m19.329s**
4 Räikkönen	**1m20.133s**
3 Coulthard	**1m20.315s**
14 Trulli	**1m20.516s**
24 Salo	**1m20.995s**
11 Villeneuve	**1m21.130s**
7 Heidfeld	**1m 21.187s**
8 Massa	**1m21.191s**
15 Button	**1m21.247s**
12 Panis	**1m21.274s**
10 Sato	**1m21.337s**
25 McNish	**1m21.382s**
20 Frentzen	**1m21.416s**
9 Fisichella	**1m21.636s**
21 Bernoldi	**1m21.780s**
16 Irvine	**1m21.851s**
23 Webber	**1m22.281s**
17 de la Rosa	**1m23.422s**

Did not qualify
22 Alex Yoong, Minardi PS02-Asiatech V10, **1m24.785s**

Circuit sections:
COPSE 135/217 ⑤
WOODCOTE 135/217 ⑥
BROOKLANDS 50/81 ②
PRIORY 95/153 ④
MAGGOTTS 130/209 ⑤
BECKETTS 95/153 ④
BRIDGE 155/250 ⑤
LUFFIELD 60/97 ②
HANGAR STRAIGHT 190/305 ⑥
ABBEY CURVE 75/121 ②
STOWE CORNER 100/161 ③
VALE 165/266 ⑤
CLUB CORNER 70/113 ②

RACE CLASSIFICATION

Pos	Driver	Nat	Car	Laps	Time
1	Michael Schumacher	D	Ferrari F2002-Ferrari V10	60	1h31m45.015s
2	Rubens Barrichello	BR	Ferrari F2002-Ferrari V10	60	+14.578s
3	Juan Pablo Montoya	CO	Williams FW24-BMW V10	60	+31.661s
4	Jacques Villeneuve	CDN	BAR 004-Honda V10		+1 lap
5	Olivier Panis	F	BAR 004-Honda V10		+1 lap
6	Nick Heidfeld	D	Sauber C21-Petronas V10		+1 lap
7	Giancarlo Fisichella	I	Jordan EJ12-Honda V10		+1 lap
8	Ralf Schumacher	D	Williams FW24-BMW V10		+1 lap
9	Felipe Massa	BR	Sauber C21-Petronas V10		+1 lap
10	David Coulthard	GB	McLaren MP4-17-Mercedes V10		+2 laps
11	Pedro de la Rosa	E	Jaguar R3-Ford Cosworth V10		+2 laps
12	Jenson Button	GB	Renault R202-Renault V10		+6 laps

Retirements		Nat	Car	Laps	Reason
Takuma Sato		J	Jordan EJ12-Honda V10	50	engine
Kimi Räikkönen		FIN	McLaren MP4-17-Mercedes V10	44	engine
Jarno Trulli		I	Renault R202-Renault V10	29	electronics
Enrique Bernoldi		BR	Arrows A23-Ford Cosworth V10	28	driveshaft
Eddie Irvine		GB	Jaguar R3-Ford Cosworth V10	23	spin
Heinz-Harald Frentzen		D	Arrows A23-Ford Cosworth V10	20	engine
Mika Salo		FIN	Toyota TF102-Toyota V10	15	transmission
Mark Webber		AUS	Minardi PS02-Asiatech V10	9	clutch/spin
Allan McNish		GB	Toyota TF102-Toyota V10	0	clutch

FASTEST LAP **R** Barrichello lap 58 1m23.083s (138.417mph/222.760kmh)

DRIVERS' CHAMPIONSHIP

1	Michael Schumacher	86
2	Rubens Barrichello	32
3	Juan Pablo Montoya	31
4	Ralf Schumacher	30
5	David Coulthard	26
6	Kimi Räikkönen	11
7	Jenson Button	10
8	Nick Heidfeld	6
	Giancarlo Fisichella	6
10	Jarno Trulli	4
	Felipe Massa	4
12	Jacques Villeneuve	3
	Eddie Irvine	3
14	Olivier Panis	2
	Mark Webber	2
	Mika Salo	2
	Heinz-Harald Frentzen	2

CONSTRUCTORS' CHAMPIONSHIP

1	Ferrari	118
2	Williams-BMW	61
3	McLaren-Mercedes	37
4	Renault	14
5	Sauber-Petronas	10
6	Jordan-Honda	6
7	BAR-Honda	5
8	Jaguar-Ford Cosworth	3
9	Minardi-Asiatech	2
	Toyota	2
	Arrows-Ford Cosworth	2

"THOSE WERE THE DAYS MY FRIEND...

...WE THOUGHT THEY'D NEVER END, WE'D SING AND DANCE FOR EVER AND A DAY. WE'D LIVE THE LIFE WE'D CHOOSE, WE'D FIGHT AND NEVER LOSE FOR WE WERE YOUNG AND SURE TO HAVE OUR WAY..."

SAGE WORDS FROM MARY HOPKIN IN October 1968, when Jackie Stewart was busy winning the US GP at Watkins Glen, Hugo Montenegro and his orchestra were in the top 20 with *The Good, The Bad and The Ugly* and Bob Beamon leapt 29ft 2.5in during the Olympic Games in Mexico City to smash the world long jump record by almost two feet. Feels like yesterday, as do many of the following landmarks, culled from the days when Roy Keane used his elbow only for writing school essays and Britain's town and city centres didn't all look the bloody same.

95 YEARS AGO/1907

AUG 7: Roger Loyer born. The Frenchman drove a Gordini in the 1954 Argentine GP, qualified 16th out of 18, retired with oil starvation and didn't race in F1 again. Quiet year, 1907. Apart from the invention of three-colour printing, that is. Oh, and 60 suffragettes being arrested after storming the British parliament to demand a right to vote.

75 YEARS AGO/1927

APR 20: Phil Hill entered planet earth. He was the first of only three people called Hill to have driven in a GP – and they have all been world champion. Wonder what odds you could have got on that on April 19, 1927?

70 YEARS AGO/1932

FEB 25: To Mr and Mrs Brooks, a son, Tony (left)... He used to skip dental lectures at university because his F1 and sports car racing commitments got in the way. Brilliant but

underrated, he won six of his 38 GPs before retiring at the end of 1961 to concentrate on developing his automotive dealership.

65 YEARS AGO/1937

AUG 30: Bruce McLaren (left) born in Auckland, New Zealand. His UK-based engineering concern began building sports cars in 1963, turned its attention to F1 in 1966 and scored its first GP success, courtesy of Bruce and the Cosworth-powered M7A, at Spa in 1968. He perished while testing one of his own CanAm cars in 1970 but had laid the foundation for one of modern F1's greatest success stories.

60 YEARS AGO/1942

APR 18: Jochen Rindt (main pic and inset) came into the world, probably at an angle few others could have achieved. Car control virtuoso scored him a long-overdue first GP win late in 1969 and added five more the following season before his death at Monza. He became the sport's only posthumous world champion.

MAY 31: Trivia question. Who drove a second Williams alongside Jacques Laffite in the 1975 Austrian GP? Answer: Swiss car dealer Jo Vonlanthen, born on this day.

55 YEARS AGO/1947

MAR 3: Otto Stuppacher's birth was probably

one of the slower variety. Entered a second-hand Tyrrell 007 for three GPs in 1976 but did not start any of them. He failed to qualify in Canada and America but could have raced in Italy. Could. Various drivers had their practice times disallowed, which promoted Otto to 26th on the grid. Unfortunately he was well on his way back home to Austria by the time all this happened and mobile phones didn't exist.

JUN 1: Ron Dennis maximised a birth canal evacuation opportunity and went on to have rather more of an impact in F1 than Herr Stuppacher.

AUG 29: Mr and Mrs Hunt welcomed new son James (left), a future budgie breeder who won the 1976 F1 title in-between serving up helpings of Trill.

50 YEARS AGO/1952
FEB 19: Stephen South born. A British rising star in the 1970s, he was axed from a potential title-winning drive with the Toleman team at the start of the 1980 European F2 season. His offence? He didn't tell his bosses that he was about to make a one-off GP appearance for McLaren at Long Beach, as stand-in for the injured Alain Prost. He failed to qualify and subsequently accepted a drive in the US-based CanAm sports car series, where he lost the lower part of one leg after a serious accident. Now unfairly consigned to the role of a footnote in F1 history, but he was *very* good.

MAR 28: Tony Brise born. He had only been in F1 a few months when he perished in a light aeroplane crash along with Graham Hill and other key members of the latter's F1 team as they returned from a test session in France on Nov 29, 1975. Like South, he was exceptionally gifted.

JUN 22: Britain's first F1 world champion Mike Hawthorn made his GP debut in Belgium. He qualified his Cooper T20-Bristol sixth of 22 and finished fourth.

AUG 17: Happy birthday Nelson Piquet. You celebrated your 50th a few months before this book was published.

45 YEARS AGO/1957
JUL 20: Cue Pathé News soundtrack. Stirling Moss (below) and Tony Brooks shared the winning Vanwall in their home GP at Aintree – the first all-British F1 success. Such occasions are inevitably accompanied by a rendition of *God Save The Queen* – but does anybody

else agree that *Jerusalem* or *I Vow To Thee My Country* would make a much better national anthem? Just wondered.

AUG 4: Juan Manuel Fangio scored his 24th and final GP win at the Nürburgring – and it was also one of his greatest after he tracked down the distant Ferraris of Mike Hawthorn and Peter Collins.

AUG 18: At 15.894 miles, Pescara in Italy (right) became the longest track to have featured in the world championship, albeit only once.

40 YEARS AGO/1962
MAY 20: Graham Hill (BRM P57) scored his first grand prix win in Holland. By the end of the year he had added three more and a world title to his CV.

JUN 17: It is a matter of record that Jim Clark didn't much like Spa, but on this day he steered his Lotus 25 to his maiden world championship success. It would be 1966 before any other driver won the Belgian GP.

JUL 8: Dan Gurney gave Porsche its first GP win at Reims, France. We're still waiting for the second.

JUL 20: Giovanna Amati born. She didn't have much impact on F1 (three attempts to qualify a Brabham early in 1992 yielded three DNQs), but she did leave her mark on the sport, mainly in the form of a bootprint on the backside of FIA F3000 rival Phil Andrews' overalls. She had a minor tantrum after accusing him of holding her up at Hockenheim in 1990.

JUL 21: Jim Clark (Lotus 25) won the final British GP to be staged at Aintree. The Merseyside track continued staging club

races into the early 1980s, but errant cars kept damaging the adjacent Grand National steeplechase course and maintenance eventually became too costly. GT racer George "Welly" Potter's Lotus Esprit once became wedged in a fence and had to be left there for the rest of the meeting because marshals had no means of shifting it (although they seem to have managed in the intervening 20-odd years).

35 YEARS AGO/1967

JAN 2: Pedro Rodriguez won the South African GP (below left) in a Cooper-Maserati, which turned out to be the final F1 success for both the British team and its Italian engine supplier. Cooper pioneered the rear-engined F1 revolution in the late 1950s and most rivals cottoned on to the idea within a couple of seasons. The Americans had it sussed by about 1967.

JUN 4: The legendary Ford-based Cosworth DFV V8 made its race debut in the Dutch GP at Zandvoort (below). Thus equipped, the Lotus 49s of Graham Hill and Jim Clark cleared off into the distance. Hill retired after 11 laps but Clark won by more than 20 seconds. By the time Michele Alboreto took the chequered flag in Detroit on Jun 5, 1983, the Cosworth had powered 155 world championship GP winners.

30 YEARS AGO/1972

FEB: *Son Of My Father* by Chicory Tip was the UK's second best-selling single, after T-Rex's *Telegram Sam*. You must remember the electric piano riff.

to be BRM's last start: the P207 subsequently reappeared but several drivers failed miserably in their efforts to make the grid.

MAY 22: Riccardo Patrese made the first of his world record 256 GP starts. He qualified his Shadow DN8 15th in Monaco (left) and finished ninth.

MAY 14: Jean-Pierre Beltoise (BRM P160B) paddled to victory in rain-drenched Monaco and gave its once-famous entrant its final GP success (above).

MAY 23: Rubens Barrichello born – but Michael Schumacher beat him to it by three years, four months and 20 days. That pattern continues today on a slightly smaller scale.

OCT 8: Future world champion Jody Scheckter (centre column, right) made his first GP start at Watkins Glen. Lining up eighth out of 30, he took his McLaren M19A to ninth place.

25 YEARS AGO/1977
JAN 9: The Wolf WR1 was one of the prettiest F1 cars of its day and made a great subject for a Tamiya model. Courtesy of a) Jody Scheckter and b) loads of retirements at the head of the field it also scored an unexpected win on its debut in the Argentine GP.

MAR 5: There was no need for marshal Jansen van Vuuren to run across Kyalami's main straight on the 23rd lap of the South African GP. The flash-fire on Renzo Zorzi's Shadow had been quelled, drama over. But van Vuuren and an associate crossed the track anyway. His colleague got there but Zorzi's team-mate Tom Pryce, unsighted, ran straight into van Vuuren, who was slowed by the fire extinguisher he carried. Both men died instantly and Britain lost one of its greatest F1 hopes.

MAR 5: BRM turned up for the South African GP with an old P201 chassis because it couldn't get the latest P207 to function. Aussie Larry Perkins managed to qualify the thing, even though it hadn't raced for more than a year, but finished five laps down because it was only running on 10 of its 12 cylinders. It was

JUL 16: A faulty water temperature gauge persuaded F1 rookie Gilles Villeneuve that he ought to bring his ageing McLaren M23 into the pits during the early stages of the British GP at Silverstone. But for that he'd have finished fourth. McLaren subsequently decided that Villeneuve wasn't the man it needed for 1978. Wrong.

JUL 16: Renault's RS01 became the first turbocharged car to start a GP. Driven by Jean-Pierre Jabouille, it expired in a cloud of steam after 16 laps.

AUG 14: Alan Jones scored an improbable victory for Shadow in the Austrian GP at the Österreichring.

OCT 23: James Hunt (McLaren M26) beat Carlos Reutemann (Ferrari 312 T2) by almost a minute in the Japanese GP at Fuji. It was to be his 10th and final world championship success.

20 YEARS AGO/1982
MAR 21: Carlos Reutemann had driven the final race of 1981 at Las Vegas as though he couldn't be arsed winning the world title, which he duly didn't. After contesting the opening two races of 1982 for Williams, he decided he couldn't be bothered racing at all. Lying third in the points table with 14 races to go, he walked away from the sport.

MAY 8: Gilles Villeneuve was pressing on particularly hard at Zolder (right). There was no way the Ferrari 126C2 was good enough for pole, but if he could beat team-mate Didier Pironi's time that would suffice. Gilles was still mad about the way he felt Pironi had duped him to win the previous race at Imola. Up ahead was Jochen Mass's March. Gilles didn't back off. Mass tried to get out of the way but

has a couple of top-class rollercoaster rides and nearby Yokkaichi has an excellent pizza restaurant. Gerhard Berger won for Ferrari (left).

10 YEARS AGO/1992

MAR 3: Lella Lombardi died. She was one of only two women to have started a world championship F1 race and made history by scoring a top-six finish in the 1975 Spanish GP.

MAR 22: The Mexican GP took place, but hasn't since. Nigel Mansell (Williams FW14B-Renault) was the last F1 victor at the Autodromo Hermanos Rodriguez. Shame it was dropped – it would be more fun than going to Germany twice a year.

AUG 16: Damon Hill finished 11th in Hungary in what turned out to be the famous Brabham marque's last GP start.

AUG 16: In the same race Nigel Mansell finished second to become the first driver since Keke Rosberg in 1982 to win the F1 title while sporting facial hair. F1's only other moustachioed champion was Graham Hill (1962 and 1968). Mansell (centre column, left) drove brilliantly that season but still refuses to concede he had any kind of car advantage. There is a technical term for this: bollocks.

AUG 30: A sprightly 23-year-old from Kerpen pranced about on top of an F1 podium for the first time, after winning the Belgian GP for Benetton. Michael Schumacher has since gone on to do this rather frequently.

the Ferrari was already gunning for the same bit of track. The impact sent the French-Canadian's car cartwheeling and he was thrown clear as it broke up. Later that evening they switched off his life-support machine. His 61 starts yielded only six wins and two pole positions; such meagre stats do not reflect his genius. The sport has not seen his like since.

SEP 25: At the age of 42 Mario Andretti started his 128th and final F1 race, in Las Vegas. He then carried on racing other stuff into his sixties.

15 YEARS AGO/1987

AUG 23: Former Renault and Ferrari F1 star Didier Pironi died after crashing during a powerboat race near the Isle of Wight. He had been forced to give up motor racing five years earlier, because of serious leg injuries sustained in a practice accident during the German GP weekend.

NOV 1: The Japanese GP returned to the calendar after a 10-year break and for the first time it was staged at Suzuka – a good call, because it is a fine track, the adjacent funfair

5 YEARS AGO/1997

AUG 10: Damon Hill came within a last-gasp hydraulic hiccough of winning the Hungarian GP in an Arrows A18-Yamaha (above). You might find a few misprints dotted around *Grand Prix Year*; oddly, this isn't one of them.

MOBIL 1 GRAND PRIX DE FRANCE

A DECADE AGO NIGEL MANSELL HAD IT ALL SEWN UP BY BUDAPEST IN MID-AUGUST. SCHUEY, THOUGH, HAD TITLE NUMBER FIVE IN THE BAG BY MAGNY-COURS IN JULY. IT'S CALLED TAKING THE MICHAEL

FINNS AIN'T WHAT THEY USED TO BE:
Déjà vu for Schuey (main shot) as Räikkönen
does a fair impersonation of predecessor Häkkinen and makes
life extremely difficult for the world champ. They are just ahead of McNish's
lapped Toyota, whose engine failure later caused the oil spill that caught Kimi
Left, Ferrari can't be bothered waiting for Rubens to get back from the airport
starts celebrating anyway

MICHAEL SCHUMACHER BEGAN HIS WEEKEND PLAYING
football for Germany's seven-a-side media team and finished it by
equalling Juan Manuel Fangio's record five world championship wins.

He hadn't expected it so soon. To make sure, he had to win with
neither Montoya nor team-mate Barrichello second. Then, when Juan
Pablo and Rubens hit trouble, Michael put a wheel over the pit lane
exit line and earned a drive-through penalty, which let in Kimi
Räikkönen. The young Finn was on course for his first grand prix
success until Allan McNish's Toyota blew up at the Adelaide Hairpin
and Kimi was caught out on the oil.

For the second race in succession poor Barrichello went nowhere
when everyone else snaked away on the formation lap. Everyone, that
is, except the financially-straitened Arrows team, whose cars had
completed one slow qualifying (or, rather, non-qualifying) run apiece
before being packed away.

The stricken Ferrari would not fire, no matter how many steering
wheels they tried or buttons they pressed. The Brazilian left the track
in a huff, only to have to come back later to join Michael's celebratory
party. Not one Doc Marten in the groin, but two…

Montoya claimed his fifth straight pole but Williams took the harder
Michelin and cloud cover on Sunday afternoon meant the Colombian
would struggle. McLaren, on the softer rubber, was the bigger threat
to Ferrari and Bridgestone in France.

Michael respectfully followed Montoya as far as the first stops, then
jumped him. In his anxiety to lead he committed his faux pas with the
white line but, such was his pace, he was nine seconds clear when he
headed in for his penalty. He emerged still third, right behind Montoya
and Räikkönen but in front of Schuey Jnr and David Coulthard. As the

STRAND AND DELIVER: clockwise from top left,
Barrichello aims for Mars while everyone else points
towards the first corner; Fisichella was less badly
damaged than his Jordan in this practice shunt but
wasn't allowed to race; Arrows boss Tom Walkinshaw
and driver Frentzen cleared off after a single
qualifying run; bird in the bush

THE STRICKEN FERRARI WOULD NOT FIRE, NO MATTER HOW MANY STEERING WHEELS THEY TRIED OR BUTTONS THEY PRESSED. THE BRAZILIAN LEFT THE TRACK IN A HUFF, ONLY TO HAVE TO COME BACK LATER TO JOIN MICHAEL'S CELEBRATORY PARTY

FINN KING AHEAD

SCHUEY, OF COURSE, IS KING. FOR MANY IN THE F1 paddock, Juan Pablo Montoya is favourite to assume Michael's mantle when he finally calls it a day. But at McLaren they don't agree.

Everyone knows Kimi Räikkönen (above) is quick but McLaren thinks he is going to be *the* man. Okay, he made a mistake in France but this is where his talent truly emerged.

"We could have had a Villeneuve or an Irvine," said McLaren MD Martin Whitmarsh about the team's decision to recruit the young Finn. "But when we were looking at the market we tried to understand capability and potential.

"Did Kimi dramatically outperform Nick Heidfeld at Sauber? No. And it would have been easier for us to go with Nick because we had supported him in F3 and F3000. We would have felt better about ourselves doing that but we took the view that Kimi's potential is higher, because his performance was on a par with Nick's and he has much less experience."

Looking at the opposition, Whitmarsh added: "Montoya is a terrific driver with some great qualifying and overtaking moves, but if you average him out he is inconsistent. As is Ralf Schumacher, in my opinion. I wouldn't want Ralf or Montoya in a team with a duff team-mate because I'm not sure they would stay honest. But such is his focus that Kimi always would.

"Fisichella is a very nice chap, with lots of raw natural talent, but again he's pretty inconsistent. He and Jarno Trulli have been terribly slow in races. Rubens is doing a great job, but is he a really tough race driver?

"Michael is a great driver but there must come a point when he has so much stacked up in the bank, such a quality of life – kids, family and so on – that barrelling into a corner with some young charger on the inside of him will make him think a bit… In a couple of years, in a head-to-head battle, Kimi will be capable of winning a championship."

Time will tell.

race reached half-distance, only three seconds covered the first five. This was great stuff.

Ultimately Montoya and Williams weren't quick enough. After the FW24s made their second pit stops, Kimi led his first grand prix with Michael on his gearbox. The Ferrari dived in five laps after Montoya; the McLaren stopped one lap later still and managed to scramble out with the red car just behind. But Coulthard was now in front. His first fuel stop had been longer and he ran for another five laps before just failing to overhaul Michael and his team-mate. But wait a minute: DC had crossed the pit exit line too, as had Ralf Schumacher and Felipe Massa.

What was going on? Massa, a man in his first season, you could understand. But Michael, Ralf and DC had driven more than 400 grands prix between them.

"At Magny-Cours the penalty line is on a curve," Coulthard explained. "It's there all weekend, of course, but in the race you're anxious to get back across to the racing line and I was just a bit too eager."

THE CAR IN THE MIDDLE OF THIS LOT IS A TOYOTA: McNish pulls in for his 55-mile service. Shame somebody forgot to tighten his sump plug properly

GUTTED, RÄIKKÖNEN SAID: "IT IS MY BEST RESULT YET BUT, AT THE SAME, IT'S ALSO THE MOST DISAPPOINTING RACE OF MY LIFE. A BIT STRANGE…"

And so the race distilled into a fight between Kimi and Michael. The Finn looked composed and the Ferrari driver's body language hinted that Michael had accepted second.

Then, with five laps to go, came McNish's blow-up. There was a yellow flag to warn following drivers about the stranded Toyota but, crucially, no red-and-yellow flag to signify a coating of oil. Kimi locked a wheel and slid straight on. By the time he gathered it all up, Michael was through. But only just. Michael nipped Kimi up the exit kerb to make sure.

Cue indignant faces on the McLaren pit wall. Hadn't Michael just overtaken under yellow?

Schuey also wondered how the stewards would read it, radioed the team and asked whether he should let Räikkönen repass. No, they said, stay put.

Technically, Kimi had been off the circuit, so Michael hadn't overtaken. What was he supposed to do? Wait for the McLaren to sort itself out and come back on?

Gutted, Räikkönen said: "It is my best result yet but, at the same, it's also the most disappointing race of my life. A bit strange…"

Was it inexperience? No. Simply the lack of an oil flag. Michael, of course, saw what happened to the Finn in the braking area and was pre-warned.

Only then did Michael start to believe in his record-equalling title. "The next five laps," he said, "were the longest of my career." He then blew away any tiny lingering suspicions about a shock retirement announcement by declaring that a Fangio-beating sixth title is very much on his agenda.

The inevitable comparisons with the great Argentine were played down. "You can't compare what modern drivers do today with what Fangio achieved in his time," Michael said. Don't believe it. Five titles and 61 grand prix wins in the modern era – any era – is a formidable achievement.

FLASHBACK

July 2 1961, Reims, France

OCCASIONALLY IN 1961 STIRLING MOSS WOULD put Rob Walker's private Lotus among the works Ferrari 156s at tracks where the driver could make a real difference. That would be Monte Carlo and the Nürburgring, then. Generally, however, this was Ferrari's year.

In France the Italian team entered a fourth car for promising youngster Giancarlo Baghetti, who was yet to be beaten in F1 after victories in non-championship races at Syracuse and Naples.

Regular works drivers Phil Hill, Wolfgang von Trips and Richie Ginther locked out the front row and Hill led initially, from Ginther and von Trips.

Ginther lost time with a spin but soon scrambled back into the top three, where there wasn't much of a race going on because Ferrari had imposed team orders (excuse us if that sounds like anything else you might have read in this book) and instructed von Trips to move to the front.

But reliability wasn't quite the same back then as it is now. The German's engine packed up after 18 laps, then Hill lost a lap when he spun and Ginther parked when his V6's oil pressure dipped.

Having started 12th, Baghetti had been in a slipstreaming pack of half a dozen cars chasing fourth place early in the race. As the works Ferraris faded, however, he found himself duelling for the lead with Dan Gurney's Porsche.

The two swapped places constantly. Gurney led into the final corner but Baghetti was on his tail and ducked out just before the flag to win by 0.1s (above). To this date no other driver has triumphed on his world championship debut. He didn't win any more GPs, mind, although he did go on to become a successful photo-journalist.

BRITAIN'S BEST-SELLING SINGLES… WHEN GIANCARLO BAGHETTI CREATED A SLICE OF F1 HISTORY	
1 EVERLY BROTHERS	Temptation
2 DEL SHANNON	Runaway
3 EDEN KANE	Well I Ask You
4 RICKY NELSON	Hello Mary Lou
5 CLIFF RICHARD	A Girl Like You

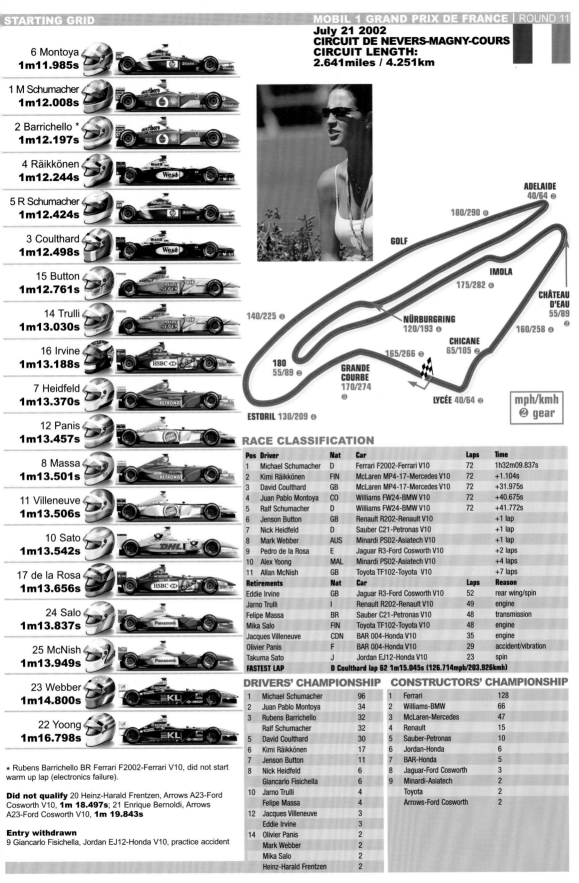

July 21 2002
CIRCUIT DE NEVERS-MAGNY-COURS
CIRCUIT LENGTH:
2.641miles / 4.251km

Starting Grid

6 Montoya
1m11.985s

1 M Schumacher
1m12.008s

2 Barrichello *
1m12.197s

4 Räikkönen
1m12.244s

5 R Schumacher
1m12.424s

3 Coulthard
1m12.498s

15 Button
1m12.761s

14 Trulli
1m13.030s

16 Irvine
1m13.188s

7 Heidfeld
1m13.370s

12 Panis
1m13.457s

8 Massa
1m13.501s

11 Villeneuve
1m13.506s

10 Sato
1m13.542s

17 de la Rosa
1m13.656s

24 Salo
1m13.837s

25 McNish
1m13.949s

23 Webber
1m14.800s

22 Yoong
1m16.798s

ADELAIDE 40/64 ②
180/290 ⑥
GOLF
IMOLA
175/282 ⑥
CHÂTEAU D'EAU 55/89 ②
140/225 ⑥
NÜRBURGRING 120/193 ⑥
160/258 ⓪
CHICANE 65/105 ②
180 55/89 ②
165/266 ⑥
GRANDE COURBE 170/274 ⑤
LYCÉE 40/64 ②
ESTORIL 130/209 ⓪

mph/kmh
② gear

* Rubens Barrichello BR Ferrari F2002-Ferrari V10, did not start warm up lap (electronics failure).

Did not qualify 20 Heinz-Harald Frentzen, Arrows A23-Ford Cosworth V10, **1m 18.497s**; 21 Enrique Bernoldi, Arrows A23-Ford Cosworth V10, **1m 19.843s**

Entry withdrawn
9 Giancarlo Fisichella, Jordan EJ12-Honda V10, practice accident

RACE CLASSIFICATION

Pos	Driver	Nat	Car	Laps	Time
1	Michael Schumacher	D	Ferrari F2002-Ferrari V10	72	1h32m09.837s
2	Kimi Räikkönen	FIN	McLaren MP4-17-Mercedes V10	72	+1.104s
3	David Coulthard	GB	McLaren MP4-17-Mercedes V10	72	+31.975s
4	Juan Pablo Montoya	CO	Williams FW24-BMW V10	72	+40.675s
5	Ralf Schumacher	D	Williams FW24-BMW V10	72	+41.772s
6	Jenson Button	GB	Renault R202-Renault V10		+1 lap
7	Nick Heidfeld	D	Sauber C21-Petronas V10		+1 lap
8	Mark Webber	AUS	Minardi PS02-Asiatech V10		+1 lap
9	Pedro de la Rosa	E	Jaguar R3-Ford Cosworth V10		+2 laps
10	Alex Yoong	MAL	Minardi PS02-Asiatech V10		+4 laps
11	Allan McNish	GB	Toyota TF102-Toyota V10		+7 laps

Retirements		Nat	Car	Laps	Reason
Eddie Irvine		GB	Jaguar R3-Ford Cosworth V10	52	rear wing/spin
Jarno Trulli		I	Renault R202-Renault V10	49	engine
Felipe Massa		BR	Sauber C21-Petronas V10	48	transmission
Mika Salo		FIN	Toyota TF102-Toyota V10	48	engine
Jacques Villeneuve		CDN	BAR 004-Honda V10	35	engine
Olivier Panis		F	BAR 004-Honda V10	29	accident/vibration
Takuma Sato		J	Jordan EJ12-Honda V10	23	spin

FASTEST LAP D Coulthard lap 62 1m15.045s (126.714mph/203.926kmh)

DRIVERS' CHAMPIONSHIP

1	Michael Schumacher	96
2	Juan Pablo Montoya	34
3	Rubens Barrichello	32
	Ralf Schumacher	32
5	David Coulthard	30
6	Kimi Räikkönen	17
7	Jenson Button	11
8	Nick Heidfeld	6
	Giancarlo Fisichella	6
10	Jarno Trulli	4
	Felipe Massa	4
12	Jacques Villeneuve	3
	Eddie Irvine	3
14	Olivier Panis	2
	Mark Webber	2
	Mika Salo	2
	Heinz-Harald Frentzen	2

CONSTRUCTORS' CHAMPIONSHIP

1	Ferrari	128
2	Williams-BMW	66
3	McLaren-Mercedes	47
4	Renault	15
5	Sauber-Petronas	10
6	Jordan-Honda	6
7	BAR-Honda	5
8	Jaguar-Ford Cosworth	3
9	Minardi-Asiatech	2
	Toyota	2
	Arrows-Ford Cosworth	2

...SER MOBIL 1 PREIS VON DEUTSCHLAND

WITH MICHAEL'S TITLE IN THE BAG, FERRARI SAID IT WOULD TURN ITS ATTENTION TOWARDS SECURING SECOND PLACE FOR RUBENS. NOT QUITE YET, THOUGH...

SCRAP MERCHANTS: the new Hockenheim might be essentially rubbish, but the layout allowed Montoya and Räikkönen to run side by side for eons (main shot). This pair will provide great entertainment in the future, but at the end of the race it was business as usual. Above, Montoya (left) and baby bro' join the obligatory Schuey-on-the-podium shot

IT WAS PARTY TIME AT THE MASSIVELY REVAMPED
Hockenheim. The faithful came to pay homage to their very own
Fangio and fittingly it was Michael – of course – who put an end to
Juan Pablo Montoya's five-race run of pole positions. It was his fourth
of the season but the first since Barcelona.

The Ferraris were rapid from first thing Friday morning and it took
a great effort from Ralf Schumacher to split the red cars on the grid.
Heading into the final qualifying runs, in fact, it was little bro' on
provisional pole.

Montoya didn't seem himself in Germany. Troubled by understeer,
he lined up fourth.

To generate a three-week summer break for the hard-worked teams,
Hockenheim followed seven days after Magny-Cours. McLaren's
stirring performance was thus fresh in the mind and few would have
laid money on the silver cars being lapped. Or on Williams giving
Ferrari a decent fight. But that's what happened.

Ferrari's stated intent was now to help Rubens Barrichello finish
second in the championship. And so, the outcome, win number 62 for
M Schumacher, will no doubt have dismayed more than a few punters
who thought they had done the smart thing *chez* William Hill.

HOME IS WHERE THE START IS: Schuey steams
into the first corner and settles the outcome of the
race with about 1h27m40s still to go (below). Trulli
being crap (above). His car unusually still in one
piece, Massa leads Button, Fisichella, Heidfeld and
Villeneuve (below right). Fernando Alonso (bottom
right) will take Button's Renault seat in 2003

FERRARI'S STATED INTENT WAS NOW TO HELP RUBENS BARRICHELLO FINISH SECOND
IN THE CHAMPIONSHIP. AND SO, THE OUTCOME, WIN NUMBER 62 FOR M SCHUMACHER,
WILL NO DOUBT HAVE DISMAYED MORE THAN A FEW PUNTERS

Amazingly, Michael had never won at Hockenheim in a Ferrari. But by half-past three on Sunday afternoon that one could be ticked off, too. For the fourth time in his career – 1995, 2000, 2001 and now 2002 – he had won nine races in a single season. The record he shared with Nigel Mansell looked most unlikely to see out the year.

"I'm sure that's in Michael's mind," said Williams technical director Patrick Head, with a grin. "The best way for him to help is by winning races with Rubens second, rather than gifting him victories. I don't think charity is part of his competitive make-up..."

Williams knew it had to aim at Schuey's performance and Head was more optimistic this time. "I'm expecting us to be strong as the race goes on," he said.

But why, given that the team had been weaker than McLaren in France?

"Our problems are all about wearing the rear tyres out too quickly, " Head explained. "It's partly a car characteristic and partly down to optimising the traction control. We think we are making progress there."

He wasn't wrong. The record books will show that Michael delighted the horn-blowing Germans by leading from lights to flag. But Williams chief operations engineer Sam Michael thinks Ralf could have beaten him.

"The race showed what a difference being on pole made. As it was, Ralf got held up a couple of times before his first pit stop and without that I think we could have got out ahead."

Ralf ran two laps longer than Michael before the first stop, but

LAUDA HEADLINE

YOU'VE HEARD THE ONE ABOUT NIKI LAUDA (ABOVE) in the Austrian TV booth? No?

Well, some while back there was a mix-up about precisely when Rubens Barrichello started his 100th grand prix. It was something to do with injuring his arm and not taking the restart after a Spa startline shunt. According to the record books, therefore, he hadn't taken part.

Explaining the concept to Lauda, someone mentioned that it was the same thing with him. Technically, the Austrian had never actually participated in the 1976 German GP at the Nürburgring, where a fierce, fiery accident almost cost him his life.

"Oh yeah?" said Lauda, "Then what the hell happened to my left ear?"

Niki's accident spelt the end for F1 at the majestic Nürburgring Nordschleife, which was already living on borrowed time as a grand prix circuit. The German GP had been run at Hockenheim in 1970 and, in 1977, it went back there. Ironically, Lauda won (see *Flashback*, page 106).

Predictably, given the challenging nature of the race's former home, nobody had a good word for its replacement. Certainly you would not have believed that, 25 years later, hacks would be scribbling wistfully about the demise of the old Hockenheim.

The flat-out blasts through the pine forests were different but many worried about mechanical failures – or contact – at 220mph-plus.

Toyota technical director Gustav Brunner has been around the block and was in no doubt that the new, shorter Hockenheim is better. He said: "There is no skill in driving at 225mph in a straight line. Some bravery perhaps, but F1 should be for the skilled, not the brave."

The new layout, designed by Hermann Tilke, allowed Messrs Montoya and Räikkönen to race side-by-side for half a lap, which can't be bad.

Medium downforce now, the circuit left unanswered the question of whether Williams-BMW could challenge Ferrari in low-downforce trim. "You'll just have to wait until Monza," Michael said with a smirk, like a schoolboy who knew all the answers.

WHEEL NERVE: McLaren's latest Ferrari-beating innovation failed to fulfil expectations

COULTHARD WAS A LAP ADRIFT IN FIFTH. HARD TO BELIEVE THIS WAS THE SAME McLAREN THAT COULD HAVE WON AT MAGNY-COURS

Schuey Jnr lost crucial time lapping Jarno Trulli, which earned the Italian a drive-through penalty.

"As well as that," Ralf said, "I had understeer on my first set of tyres." There was also a communications problem with the Williams lollipop man at that second stop, which cost more time. Then, four laps from the end, he was called in to have some air added to the engine's pneumatic valve system. Gallingly, that dropped him to third behind Montoya.

And Rubens?

He had first call on the T-car for the rest of the season – and needed it when his race chassis developed a transmission problem as he joined the grid. Then, running a strong third, his fuel flap refused to open at his second stop, which lost him 15 seconds. He would not have beaten either Schumacher on pace but, given Ralf's problems, he would have been second rather than fourth.

Montoya's hopes took a knock when Räikkönen outfoxed him at Turn Two on the opening lap. The McLaren couldn't keep pace with the leading trio and Montoya was stuck behind the Finn for 10 laps. But they gave us superb entertainment, running side-by-side for half a lap.

It put you in mind of René Arnoux versus Gilles Villeneuve at Dijon in 1979. And there were more GV memories when Kimi's left rear Michelin blew and the Finn carried on to prove that you really can drive back to the pits on the left rear rim. Michelin suspected that Kimi's tyre punctured on debris and he did another 15 laps before spinning off at the final corner.

David Coulthard was a lap adrift in fifth. Hard to believe this was the same McLaren that could have won at Magny-Cours. The team never achieved a workable chassis/tyre balance all weekend.

Michael had bagged 20 points in seven days and Budapest, scene of one of his most memorable wins, was next up.

FLASHBACK

July 31 1977, Hockenheim, Germany

THE GERMAN GP'S SWITCH FROM THE DAUNTING, 14-mile Nürburgring to fast-but-featureless Hockenheim was a retrograde step in the eyes of purists, but essential in the name of safety.

One year earlier Niki Lauda's fearful accident (see also sidebar, page 105) was the catalyst that finally consigned the 'Ring' to the annals of F1 history.

There were many talking points during the 1977 race – not least Lauda's victory on the first anniversary of the shunt that almost killed him. It was the Ferrari driver's second of the year and put him 10 points clear of closest world title rival Jody Scheckter (Wolf WR1).

A much greater statistical curiosity, however, was the performance of German touring car racer Hans Heyer (above), who had been drafted into the ATS Penske team for the weekend. History recalls that he retired after nine laps with broken gear linkage… and also that he was 27th fastest in qualifying at a circuit licensed to accommodate only 24 cars.

Before the start, he quietly parked up close to the track and waited for the rest of the field to roar away. While everyone was watching the legitimate qualifiers streaming towards the first turn, Heyer calmly drove on to the circuit and joined in, to enthusiastic cheers from the stands.

It wasn't the only rule he broke during the weekend, either. The regulations forbade GP drivers from taking part in any other events within 24 hours of the start, but the previous day Heyer had contested a support race right under the noses of Hockenheim officials. Not that they had realised he was planning to do the GP…

Sadly, that gear linkage failure stopped him before further anarchy could occur.

BRITAIN'S BEST-SELLING SINGLES… WHEN HANS HEYER MADE HIS ONE – AND, FUNNILY ENOUGH, ONLY – F1 START	
1 HOT CHOCOLATE	So You Win Again
2 ELP	Fanfare For The Common Man
3 GLADYS KNIGHT & THE PIPS	Baby Don't Change Your Mind
4 BONEY M	Ma Baker
5 DONNA SUMMER	I Feel Love

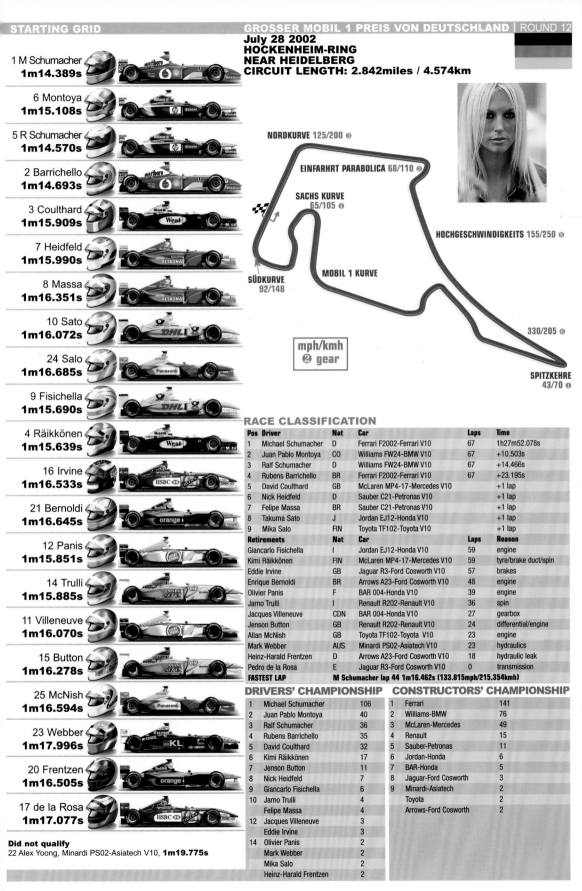

July 28 2002
HOCKENHEIM-RING
NEAR HEIDELBERG
CIRCUIT LENGTH: 2.842miles / 4.574km

1 M Schumacher
1m14.389s

6 Montoya
1m15.108s

5 R Schumacher
1m14.570s

2 Barrichello
1m14.693s

3 Coulthard
1m15.909s

7 Heidfeld
1m15.990s

8 Massa
1m16.351s

10 Sato
1m16.072s

24 Salo
1m16.685s

9 Fisichella
1m15.690s

4 Räikkönen
1m15.639s

16 Irvine
1m16.533s

21 Bernoldi
1m16.645s

12 Panis
1m15.851s

14 Trulli
1m15.885s

11 Villeneuve
1m16.070s

15 Button
1m16.278s

25 McNish
1m16.594s

23 Webber
1m17.996s

20 Frentzen
1m16.505s

17 de la Rosa
1m17.077s

Did not qualify
22 Alex Yoong, Minardi PS02-Asiatech V10, **1m19.775s**

NORDKURVE 125/200 ③

EINFAHRT PARABOLICA 68/110 ②

SACHS KURVE 65/105 ①

HOCHGESCHWINDIGKEITS 155/250 ⑤

SÜDKURVE 92/148

MOBIL 1 KURVE

330/205 ⑥

mph/kmh ② gear

SPITZKEHRE 43/70 ①

RACE CLASSIFICATION

Pos	Driver	Nat	Car	Laps	Time
1	Michael Schumacher	D	Ferrari F2002-Ferrari V10	67	1h27m52.078s
2	Juan Pablo Montoya	CO	Williams FW24-BMW V10	67	+10.503s
3	Ralf Schumacher	D	Williams FW24-BMW V10	67	+14.466s
4	Rubens Barrichello	BR	Ferrari F2002-Ferrari V10	67	+23.195s
5	David Coulthard	GB	McLaren MP4-17-Mercedes V10		+1 lap
6	Nick Heidfeld	D	Sauber C21-Petronas V10		+1 lap
7	Felipe Massa	BR	Sauber C21-Petronas V10		+1 lap
8	Takuma Sato	J	Jordan EJ12-Honda V10		+1 lap
9	Mika Salo	FIN	Toyota TF102-Toyota V10		+1 lap

Retirements	Nat	Car	Laps	Reason
Giancarlo Fisichella	I	Jordan EJ12-Honda V10	59	engine
Kimi Räikkönen	FIN	McLaren MP4-17-Mercedes V10	59	tyre/brake duct/spin
Eddie Irvine	GB	Jaguar R3-Ford Cosworth V10	57	brakes
Enrique Bernoldi	BR	Arrows A23-Ford Cosworth V10	48	engine
Olivier Panis	F	BAR 004-Honda V10	39	engine
Jarno Trulli	I	Renault R202-Renault V10	36	spin
Jacques Villeneuve	CDN	BAR 004-Honda V10	27	gearbox
Jenson Button	GB	Renault R202-Renault V10	24	differential/engine
Allan McNish	GB	Toyota TF102-Toyota V10	23	engine
Mark Webber	AUS	Minardi PS02-Asiatech V10	23	hydraulics
Heinz-Harald Frentzen	D	Arrows A23-Ford Cosworth V10	18	hydraulic leak
Pedro de la Rosa	E	Jaguar R3-Ford Cosworth V10	0	transmission
FASTEST LAP		M Schumacher lap 44 1m16.462s (133.815mph/215.354kmh)		

DRIVERS' CHAMPIONSHIP

1	Michael Schumacher	106
2	Juan Pablo Montoya	40
3	Ralf Schumacher	36
4	Rubens Barrichello	35
5	David Coulthard	32
6	Kimi Räikkönen	17
7	Jenson Button	11
8	Nick Heidfeld	7
9	Giancarlo Fisichella	6
10	Jarno Trulli	4
	Felipe Massa	4
12	Jacques Villeneuve	3
	Eddie Irvine	3
14	Olivier Panis	2
	Mark Webber	2
	Mika Salo	2
	Heinz-Harald Frentzen	2

CONSTRUCTORS' CHAMPIONSHIP

1	Ferrari	141
2	Williams-BMW	76
3	McLaren-Mercedes	49
4	Renault	15
5	Sauber-Petronas	11
6	Jordan-Honda	6
7	BAR-Honda	5
8	Jaguar-Ford Cosworth	3
9	Minardi-Asiatech	2
	Toyota	2
	Arrows-Ford Cosworth	2

MARLBORO MAGYAR NAGYDIJ

RUBENS BARRICHELLO TOOK POLE POSITION AND LED FROM LIGHTS TO FLAG IN HUNGARY. AND SCHUEY SEEMED QUITE PREPARED TO LET HIM

HARMONY HERR SPRAY the Schueys flank Rubens after Michael's expertly-judged just-did-enough-to-make-sure-I-didn't-win performance. Champagne wasn't the only thing brimming over (above). The rising Danube put several parts of central Budapest on flood alert

WITH MICHAEL'S TITLE WRAPPED UP AND A SCHUEY HOME
win at Hockenheim in the locker, attention switched to Rubens in Hungary. Ferrari's targets were now to secure the championship for constructors and make sure Barrichello completed a team one-two in the drivers' division.

Schuey is always blindingly quick around the Hungaroring. Well, apart from 1997, when he nearly suffered a cardiac as Damon Hill's Arrows-Yamaha outbraked him into Turn One. But that was down to tyres. After intensive counselling he was able to resume a highly successful career…

In 2001 Michael took the Hungaroring pole and was 0.8s quicker than Rubens. A lap 0.05s slower than his team-mate this time was surprising, perhaps even a little suspicious.

Some put it down to superb driving from Rubens, who maximised the F2002's set-up via scrubbed fronts/used rears while Michael went for new Bridgestones all round. Well, maybe, but that's hardly a ground-breaking concept in Budapest and someone who should know reckons that Michael could have had the pole if he'd wanted it.

So why didn't he? Well, if the intention was to help Rubens, the pole here is even more significant than in Monte Carlo. How so? Because

CLONE ARRANGER: overtaking was rendered even more difficult in Hungary (below) after grid girls picketed the start straight in protest at London tube drivers getting far too much money for running a crap service. Above, with Yoong gone for two races, Minardi called up young gun Davidson

IN 2001 MICHAEL TOOK THE HUNGARORING POLE AND WAS 0.8S QUICKER THAN RUBENS. A LAP 0.05S SLOWER THAN HIS TEAM-MATE THIS TIME WAS SURPRISING, PERHAPS EVEN A LITTLE SUSPICIOUS

overtaking is just about as difficult and the Hungaroring is so dusty that he who qualifies second is invariably beaten off the line by he who qualifies third, on the clean side of the track.

If Rubens had been second on the grid, therefore, he would have emerged from Turn One behind a Williams or a McLaren and Ferrari's race plans could be torn up.

As it was, Michael emerged second by leaning heavily on his brother. At that moment the Hungarian GP was over as a motor race.

When David Coulthard and McLaren won Monte Carlo, they said their next-best chance would come here, a similarly high-downforce venue. Instead, we got the team's worst qualifying performance of the season: 10th and 11th. Disappointingly, in the light of Monaco, Michelin had made a surprisingly conservative tyre selection and McLaren couldn't get any heat in its rears. Okay, the ambient temperature climbed helpfully on Sunday afternoon, but from back there Ron Dennis's men were in deep trouble.

"We were surprised at Michelin's choice and I think William was, too," Dennis said. "Normally we see Williams running on the harder, primary tyre and we use the softer option. But here the primary is way out of range and we couldn't get our car to work on the option during qualifying. The Williams is a different animal and is more aggressive on its tyres."

They were right about Sunday. Räikkönen lapped within three hundredths of Barrichello's best and DC was comfortably quicker than Ralf, but from so far back it didn't matter.

Räikkönen spent the first 20-plus laps trundling round behind Juan Pablo Montoya. Among the Colombian's pet hates, he lists the Hungaroring and understeer. Put both together and you got a qualifying lap fully a second adrift of his team-mate.

The first pit stops came after about 30 laps. In Hungary you do a

PARTY POLITICS

HUNGARY. DULL AS DITCH WATER ON THE TRACK, very bloody funny off it. For a few weeks there had been whispers about Eddie Jordan (above right) enticing Ford back as an official engine supplier.

Sensitive stuff, this. The Ford-Cosworth V10 is more than a decent unit and the thought of what Giancarlo Fisichella might do in a simple Jordan chassis with a Cossie in the back was no doubt enough to traumatise Niki Lauda (above left), boss of the engine supplier's official partner Jaguar.

There were complications, as always. Jordan and Honda had to split in such a way that honour was maintained. More than that, Fisi's contract dictated that Jordan needed to have a works engine or he was free to look at options elsewhere.

Lauda was sure the Jordan/Ford deal wasn't going to happen and said that Arrows' ongoing problems – the team didn't show up at all in Hungary – meant there was a spare supply of "customer" Cosworths available. In an FIA press conference Niki said that it was up to EJ if he wanted to "dump" his Hondas. The words "dump" and "customer" were not well received by Eddie.

On Sunday morning Jordan announced his Ford deal. Nobody representing the Blue Oval said anything official until Monza, a month later. "Looks like we've been had over by the bloody leprechaun," Lauda is alleged to have muttered. They aren't big on political correctness in Austria.

It was all good stuff, as was BAR test driver Anthony Davidson's F1 debut for Minardi, where he replaced the out-of-form Alex Yoong for two races.

He qualified about half a second adrift of highly-rated team-mate Mark Webber and made his first mistake of the weekend with just 14 laps to go, when he spun off at Turn Nine. But not before he'd set the 14th quickest race lap, faster than Webber, Jenson Button, both Toyotas and Pedro de la Rosa.

STONE CHIPS WITH EVERYTHING: McNish found some parts of the track were almost as dusty as the Tarmac (top). Above, does my bum look big in this? No

HE ALLOWED HIMSELF TO FALL FOUR SECONDS ADRIFT THEN, IN ONE LAP, WAS BACK ON RUBENS' GEARBOX WITH A FASTEST RACE LAP OF 1m16.20s

quicker time on used tyres/light fuel than with new rubber/heavy fuel so it's an advantage to stay out later. As Rubens was the leading Ferrari, it was Michael who came in first. Even so, Schumacher's out lap was so fast that he almost overcame the disadvantage. Almost, but not quite. As Rubens came out of the pits, Michael was almost alongside into Turn One but then flicked neatly in behind.

Asked afterwards whether there was ever a chance that he might have found a way by, Schumacher grinned: "That wasn't the intention, honestly…" It was the same story second time round and Michael's precision was quite breathtaking. A job with the Red Arrows – the other ones – awaits upon retirement.

In case anyone hadn't quite grasped the situation, Michael dropped another huge clue. As the Ferraris cruised during the final laps of a tedious afternoon, he allowed himself to fall four seconds adrift then, in one lap, was back on Rubens' gearbox with a fastest race lap of 1m16.20s.

"At Silverstone," Michael explained, "Rubens was behind me and we weren't pushing any more but he put in the fastest lap of the race. We were actually in the slowing-down stage, so I asked him, 'When did you do that?' So, today, I got on the radio and asked Ross Brawn what the fastest time was and he said that it was a 1m 16.8s for Rubens. I thought, 'Okay, I'll pay him back!' I needed that gap to do such a lap."

FLASHBACK

August 16 1998, Budapest, Hungary

THE TIGHT, TWISTY HUNGARORING? YOU NEED oodles of downforce and a car capable of changing direction faster than a politician. In the summer of 1998 there was only one answer: an Adrian Newey-designed McLaren. Sure enough, Mika Häkkinen and David Coulthard locked out the front row. Michael Schumacher and Ferrari were a menace, sure, but the Finn was almost four tenths quicker than Schuey. In Hungary, of all places, it would take something special to topple the Silver Arrows.

McLaren began the race intending to run a conventional two-stop strategy. So did Ferrari… until a bulb lit up between technical director Ross Brawn's ears.

Michael followed Mika and David in the early stages of the race and came in to refuel for the first time on lap 25 of 77. A standard two-stopper… except that he was given precious little juice. Returning to the track light and nimble, he was relentlessly fast and inch perfect. Still running third, he stopped for the second time on lap 43 before peeling back onto the track. Suddenly there was a crackle on the radio. Brawn: "You,ve got 19 laps to make up 25 seconds. Do it." Being Michael, he did.

McLaren brought Coulthard and Häkkinen in within the next three laps and gave both enough fuel to get to the end of the race. Heavy, that, and sluggish. Michael took the lead on lap 47, when Häkkinen pitted for the second time, and built up such an advantage that he had time to make another stop and still emerge five seconds clear. Coulthard was second; Häkkinen slipped to sixth with broken front suspension.

Michael drove the last 50-odd laps as though it were a qualifying session. It was probably his finest performance.

BRITAIN'S BEST-SELLING SINGLES... WHEN ROSS BRAWN WON THE HUNGARIAN GRAND PRIX	
1 SPICE GIRLS	Viva Forever
2 BOYZONE	No Matter What
3 PRAS MICHEL	Ghetto Superstar
4 ANOTHER LEVEL	Freak Me
5 ACE OF BASE	Life Is A Flower

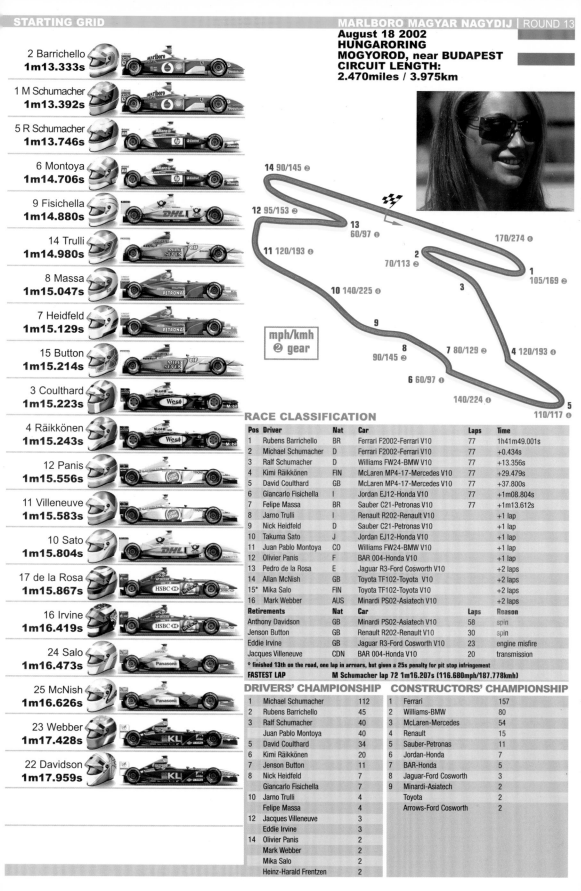

August 18 2002
HUNGARORING
MOGYOROD, near BUDAPEST
CIRCUIT LENGTH:
2.470miles / 3.975km

2 Barrichello
1m13.333s

1 M Schumacher
1m13.392s

5 R Schumacher
1m13.746s

6 Montoya
1m14.706s

9 Fisichella
1m14.880s

14 Trulli
1m14.980s

8 Massa
1m15.047s

7 Heidfeld
1m15.129s

15 Button
1m15.214s

3 Coulthard
1m15.223s

4 Räikkönen
1m15.243s

12 Panis
1m15.556s

11 Villeneuve
1m15.583s

10 Sato
1m15.804s

17 de la Rosa
1m15.867s

16 Irvine
1m16.419s

24 Salo
1m16.473s

25 McNish
1m16.626s

23 Webber
1m17.428s

22 Davidson
1m17.959s

14 90/145 ②
12 95/153 ②
13 60/97 ①
11 120/193 ①
170/274 ②
2 70/113 ②
1 105/169 ②
10 140/225 ①
3
9
8 90/145 ②
7 80/129 ②
4 120/193 ①
6 60/97 ①
140/224 ①
5 110/117 ①

mph/kmh
② gear

RACE CLASSIFICATION

Pos	Driver	Nat	Car	Laps	Time
1	Rubens Barrichello	BR	Ferrari F2002-Ferrari V10	77	1h41m49.001s
2	Michael Schumacher	D	Ferrari F2002-Ferrari V10	77	+0.434s
3	Ralf Schumacher	D	Williams FW24-BMW V10	77	+13.356s
4	Kimi Räikkönen	FIN	McLaren MP4-17-Mercedes V10	77	+29.457s
5	David Coulthard	GB	McLaren MP4-17-Mercedes V10	77	+37.800s
6	Giancarlo Fisichella	I	Jordan EJ12-Honda V10	77	+1m08.804s
7	Felipe Massa	BR	Sauber C21-Petronas V10	77	+1m13.612s
8	Jarno Trulli	I	Renault R202-Renault V10		+1 lap
9	Nick Heidfeld	D	Sauber C21-Petronas V10		+1 lap
10	Takuma Sato	J	Jordan EJ12-Honda V10		+1 lap
11	Juan Pablo Montoya	CO	Williams FW24-BMW V10		+1 lap
12	Olivier Panis	F	BAR 004-Honda V10		+1 lap
13	Pedro de la Rosa	E	Jaguar R3-Ford Cosworth V10		+2 laps
14	Allan McNish	GB	Toyota TF102-Toyota V10		+2 laps
15*	Mika Salo	FIN	Toyota TF102-Toyota V10		+2 laps
16	Mark Webber	AUS	Minardi PS02-Asiatech V10		+2 laps
Retirements		**Nat**	**Car**	**Laps**	**Reason**
Anthony Davidson		GB	Minardi PS02-Asiatech V10	58	spin
Jenson Button		GB	Renault R202-Renault V10	30	spin
Eddie Irvine		GB	Jaguar R3-Ford Cosworth V10	23	engine misfire
Jacques Villeneuve		CDN	BAR 004-Honda V10	20	transmission

* finished 13th on the road, one lap in arrears, but given a 25s penalty for pit stop infringement

FASTEST LAP   M Schumacher lap 72 1m16.207s (116.680mph/187.778kmh)

DRIVERS' CHAMPIONSHIP			**CONSTRUCTORS' CHAMPIONSHIP**	
1	Michael Schumacher	112	1 Ferrari	157
2	Rubens Barrichello	45	2 Williams-BMW	80
3	Ralf Schumacher	40	3 McLaren-Mercedes	54
	Juan Pablo Montoya	40	4 Renault	15
5	David Coulthard	34	5 Sauber-Petronas	11
6	Kimi Räikkönen	20	6 Jordan-Honda	7
7	Jenson Button	11	7 BAR-Honda	5
8	Nick Heidfeld	7	8 Jaguar-Ford Cosworth	3
	Giancarlo Fisichella	7	9 Minardi-Asiatech	2
10	Jarno Trulli	4	Toyota	2
	Felipe Massa	4	Arrows-Ford Cosworth	2
12	Jacques Villeneuve	3		
	Eddie Irvine	3		
14	Olivier Panis	2		
	Mark Webber	2		
	Mika Salo	2		
	Heinz-Harald Frentzen	2		

RISING FROM THE CRÈCHES

HOW HARD IS IT GETTING INTO FORMULA ONE NOWADAYS? PUT IT THIS WAY. BY LAST AUGUST ALL THE TOP F1 SEATS FOR 2003 WERE PRETTY MUCH SPOKEN FOR. MINARDI HAD ABOUT 20 CANDIDATES FOR ITS TWO VACANCIES; ARROWS HAD TWO SEATS BUT NO ENGINES AND LITTLE CHANCE OF SURVIVAL. YOUNG DRIVERS CONTINUE TO MAKE HUGE PERSONAL SACRIFICES IN PURSUIT OF SUCH ELUSIVE GOALS, HOWEVER. HERE ARE SOME OF THE BEST OF THE CURRENT CROP, IN ALPHABETICAL ORDER

FABIO CARBONE (BRA), right

2002 achievements: Avon Rookie of the Year in British F3 Championship. More impressively, beat a high-class international field to win the Marlboro Masters at Zandvoort

F1 prospects: above average – one of the best of the Brazilian new wave. If rather average South Americans can make it to grand prix racing (case for the prosecution: Pedro Diniz, Gaston Mazzacane, Esteban Tuero etc etc), then Carbone shouldn't have too much trouble (assuming there are any seats available ever again)

ADAM CARROLL (GBR)

2002 achievements: won British F3 Scholarship Class title

F1 prospects: too early to say. Second-string F3 category much stronger than it used to be, but the manner in which the Northern Irishman managed to get among the main title contenders bodes well... if British industry can be bothered sticking its hand in its pocket to support worthy causes. Visited the Japanese GP to begin making F1 contacts. Smart move

JAMES COURTNEY (AUS), below

2002 achievements: runner-up in British F3 series

F1 prospects: possibly fading. Had already had one unsuccessful tilt at the F3 title and was expected to succeed this time after signing for defending champion Carlin Motorsport. Accident while

testing Jaguar F1 car mid-season knocked the stuffing out of him and caused him to miss a couple of races. Not too late to regain career momentum of two years ago, when he swept up in British Formula Ford, but can't afford another season like this

RENAUD DERLOT (FRA)

2002 achievements: French F3 front-runner

F1 prospects: probably slim, because France – which once had a steady stream of top-class F1 graduates – appears to have given up backing young drivers. Was vying with Tristan Gommendy for the national F3 title when this book closed for press, but series insiders say Derlot is the man to watch

CHRISTIAN ENGLAND (GBR)

2002 achievements: runner-up in British Formula Ford Championship

F1 prospects: give him time. Recent tradition dictates that the works Van Diemen team is the one to beat in the British FF series. That JLR driver England kept the title contest alive until the final meeting speaks volumes for his potential. Trouble is, there are so many junior series nowadays that it's impossible to know whether any of the leading runners are any good until they get further up the ladder

ROBBIE KERR (GBR), left

2002 achievements: British F3 champion

F1 prospects: passable. Reigning F3 Scholarship Class champ stepped up to top division and was expected to be a front-runner... although few predicted that he'd go the whole hog. Alan Docking Racing is a good, solid team but hasn't put together a title challenge quite like this in recent years. Kerr was probably Hinckley's highest-achieving international sportsman in 2002

HEIKKI KOVALAINEN (FIN), main pic

2002 achievements: third in British F3 series

F1 prospects: strong. Has lots of Ks and Ns in his name, which seems to be as much a catalyst for promotion in racing as it is in rallying nowadays. Scored five victories in British F3 series. Highly regarded

ROB NGUYEN (AUS), left

2002 achievements: 14th in the FIA F3000 series, but bear with us

F1 prospects: much better than you'd imagine, given the above. Born in Brisbane to Vietnamese parents, Nguyen first tested a single-seater in November 2000 as a reward for doing well in his university exams. Despite having previously done nothing more exciting than indoor karting, he absolutely flew and was snapped up to race in the German-based Formula VW series in 2001. He did well there and, with all of nine races under his belt, opted to move up to F3000. He scored points in his sixth race and qualified fourth at Monza. Has colossal potential

GARY PAFFETT (GBR), left
2002 achievements: German F3 champion
F1 prospects: good. The first Brit to lift the F3 title in Germany, where competition is just as strong as it is in the UK. Vitantonio Liuzzi was one of the guys he had to beat – and Italians regard him as the most likely man to break a world title drought that stretches back to Alberto Ascari in 1953. Things didn't go all Paffett's way during the season, but he was brilliant when it mattered most

BJÖRN WIRDHEIM (SWE), left
2002 achievements: fourth – and top rookie – in the FIA F3000 series
F1 prospects: decent. Michael Schumacher has never raced against a Swede in F1 and it's about time that changed (none has contested a grand prix since Stefan Johansson qualified his Footwork-Porsche in Canada, 1991). In his first F3000 season Wirdheim established himself as a regular front-runner, a terrific overtaker and, in the seasonal finale, a race winner

WHERE ARE THEY NOW?
GPY HAS BEEN POINTING OUT DRIVERS TO WATCH SINCE 1997, BUT WE HAVEN'T ALWAYS GOT THINGS RIGHT. HERE'S WHAT OUR TIPS FROM THE PAST SIX SEASONS WERE UP TO IN 2002

1997
SOHEIL AYARI (FRA)
Then: FIA F3000 race winner
Now: front-runner in the French touring car series

JAMIE DAVIES (GBR)
Then: FIA F3000 title contender
Now: reinventing himself in the British GT Championship

NICK HEIDFELD (GER)
Then: German F3 champion
Now: has three seasons of F1 under his belt and stays with Sauber in 2003

JONNY KANE (GBR)
Then: British F3 champion
NOW: member of the MG team at Le Mans, but generally underemployed

NICOLAS MINASSIAN (FRA)
Then: British F3 runner-up, thrower of stones at rivals who pushed him off the track
Now: has fallen off the single-seater ladder after disappointing spell in US-based CART series, but won the 2002 ASCAR title (for American-style stock cars competing on European banked ovals, of which there are only a couple at present)

JUAN PABLO MONTOYA (COL), left
Then: FIA F3000 runner-up
Now: qualified on pole position for as many grands prix as Michael Schumacher in 2002, but failed to win any of them. Tied to Williams-BMW until the end of 2004

JÖRG MÜLLER (GER)
Then: talented former FIA F3000 champ casting for work
Now: talented former FIA F3000 champ winning races for BMW in the European Touring Car Championship

JASON WATT (DEN)
Then: FIA F3000 race winner
Now: one of the most uplifting tales in modern motor sport. Paralysed from the waist down after a motorcycle accident late in 1999, he has since returned to racing in the Danish touring car series at the wheel of a specially adapted Peugeot. In 2002 he guided his 307 GTi to championship success and is looking forward to racing again at international level. All-round top bloke

MAX WILSON (BRA)
Then: FIA F3000 front-runner
Now: cashflow crisis stemmed his CART career so he's racing V8 touring cars in Australia

RICARDO ZONTA (BRA)
Then: FIA F3000 champion
Now: failed to make the most of several promising F1 opportunities but had just clinched the Spain-based Formula Nissan V6 title as we closed for press

1998
Er, we didn't get round to running the feature, for reasons science is powerless to explain

1999
WESTLEY BARBER (GBR)
Then: promising rising star in F3
Now: British Formula Ford champion... has taken a couple of steps back in an effort to move forward, which he is young enough to get away with

LUCIANO BURTI (BRA)
Then: British F3 runner-up
Now: Ferrari test driver, having failed to impress on F1 frontline with either Jaguar or Prost

JENSON BUTTON (GBR), left
Then: British F3 front-runner
Now: millionaire with yachts, cars, mansions, model girlfriend, goatee beard etc etc. Sensation with Williams in 2000; faltered with Benetton-Renault in 2001; reputation partially restored with Renault in 2002; committed to BAR-Honda until at least the end of 2004

PETER DUMBRECK (GBR)
Then: front-runner in Japan-based Formula Nippon series, member of Mercedes-Benz aerobatic team at Le Mans
Now: still driving for Merc in Germany's DTM touring car series... but they made him race a 2001-spec C-class and might as well have given him a 12-year-old 200 diesel

DARIO FRANCHITTI (GBR)
Then: front-runner in US-based CART series
Now: front-runner in US-based CART series who happens to be married to Hollywood star Ashley Judd; switching to the oval-only Indy Racing League in 2003

MARC HYNES (GBR)
Then: British F3 champion
Now: more or less vanished off the face of the sport

BRUNO JUNQUEIRA (BRA)
Then: FIA F3000 front-runner
Now: reasonably regular winner in CART

DARREN MANNING (GBR)
Then: All-Japan F3 champion
Now: stumbled after intermittently promising two-year spell in FIA F3000 and has established himself as an ASCAR front-runner. Also holds world land speed record for driving in reverse

FRANCK MONTAGNY (FRA)
Then: FIA F3000 front-runner
Now: title contender in Formula Nissan V6 series

STÉPHANE SARRAZIN (FRA)
Then: FIA F3000 race winner
Now: made one F1 start for Minardi in 1999 and acquitted himself well, but was axed by McLaren F3000 team the following year for mouthing off in the press. His career hasn't really recovered since, although Toyota uses him for F1 test work

2000

FERNANDO ALONSO (ESP)
Then: FIA F3000 race winner
Now: showed great flair during 2001 F1 season with Minardi; joins Renault in 2003 after spending last season as its test driver

SÉBASTIEN BOURDAIS (FRA)
Then: FIA F3000 front-runner
Now: FIA F3000 champion

JONATHAN COCHET (FRA)
Then: French F3 champion
Now: former French F3 champion who hasn't got very far; racing in Formula Nissan V6 series

ANTONIO PIZZONIA (BRA), left
Then: British F3 champion
Now: FIA F3000 front-runner and Williams-BMW F1 tester. F3000 results haven't been great, but Williams insiders say he is faster over a race distance than Juan Pablo Montoya

KIMI RÄIKKÖNEN (FIN), left
Then: British Formula Renault champion
Now: monosyllabic superstar who is tied to a long-term McLaren contract

TOMAS SCHECKTER (RSA)
Then: British F3 and FIA F3000 front-runner, plus Jaguar F1 test driver
Now: rebuilding his career in the Indy Racing League after losing Jaguar job when he was caught in the red-light district of Northampton

2001

FELIPE MASSA (BRA)
Then: Euro F3000 champ about to join Sauber
Now: about to leave Sauber, future sadly uncertain. Team has dumped him in favour of Heinz-Harald Frentzen for 2003. There's progression

GIORGIO PANTANO (ITA), left
Then: FIA F3000 race winner
Now: FIA F3000 runner-up with an eye on a CART deal

TAKUMA SATO (JAP), left
Then: British F3 champion
Now: the reason TV audiences have shot up by more in Japan this year than they've shot down everywhere else. Has contract with Jordan for 2003, but won't necessarily stay because F1 paperwork tends to be less than fully binding

RICARDO SPERAFICO (BRA)
Then: FIA F3000 front-runner
Now: FIA F3000 front-runner, but a bit less frequently so

MARK WEBBER (AUS), left
Then: FIA F3000 runner-up
Now: responsible for Minardi's best result since France 1994 and on the shopping list of several other F1 teams, notably Jaguar (a deal that might have happened by the time this is printed; if it doesn't he'll probably stay put)

JUSTIN WILSON (GBR)
Then: FIA F3000 champion
Now: biding his time in Formula Nissan V6 series, but completed impressive Minardi F1 test and has also emerged as a candidate to land a job with title-winning CART team Newman/Haas, whose star turn Cristiano da Matta has been nicked by Toyota for 2003

FOSTER'S BELGIAN GRAND PRIX

WOULD FORMULA ONE HAVE BEEN ANY
MORE OF A SPECTACLE IN 2002 IF FERRARI
ALLOWED ITS DRIVERS TO RACE? ER, NOT
IF SPA WAS ANYTHING TO GO BY

DEMON HILL: for all that drivers might have been
comfortably flat out through Eau Rouge (above) in
2002, it remains one of the most exciting component
parts of the F1 season. Left, two people who weren't
exactly stretched on Sunday September 1

RUBENS' MASTERCLASS: except that Schuey is probably about halfway to Les Combes by now. Barrichello leads Kimi, the Williams twins and the rest of the also-rans into La Source on lap one (above). From left, above: Panis dives inside Sato; cash-strapped Arrows heads for home without turning a wheel; Villeneuve at speed

IF ANYONE HAD ANY DOUBTS, MICHAEL SHOWED US ALL AT SPA. THERE WERE STILL A FEW SOULS OUT THERE WHO THOUGHT RUBENS BEAT HIM FAIR AND SQUARE IN HUNGARY...

FORGET SANDBAGGING, SPA 2002 HAD MICHAEL Schumacher written all over it.

This year's Belgian GP marked the 10th anniversary of the German's maiden F1 success and it gave him his 10th win of the campaign – another seasonal record to add to a growing list. And it is also his favourite circuit, one he says feels like a comfortable sofa. The upshot was that nobody got remotely near him all weekend. It was the first time Michael had been to Belgium with a car advantage and he duly took his first Spa pole, a stat that surprised even the man himself. Then he simply checked out.

You had to feel a little sorry for Ferrari. The man in the street was becoming disillusioned. It was either a walkover or a fix. F1 revenue is linked to TV figures and some of the viewers were switching off. If Ferrari tried to engineer excitement there was public outcry. If it let things run their natural course, that was a turn-off too. Mind you, there's

many a team principal who'd have killed to share the Scuderia's problems. "I think that if any team dominates, the thing you must have is an ability for team-mates to race," said McLaren boss Ron Dennis. He pointed to 1988 when McLaren won 15 of the 16 races and would have had a clean sweep had a dozing Jean-Louis Schlesser not tripped up Ayrton Senna at Monza. We all knew which team was going to win but the contest between Senna and Alain Prost was sporting rivalry to rank with Ali/Frazier and Borg/McEnroe. Gripping stuff.

But if you let Michael Schumacher and Rubens Barrichello drive a grand prix flat out from lights to flag, what was going to happen? No disrespect to Rubens but, if anyone had any doubts, Michael showed us all at Spa. There were still a few souls out there who thought Rubens beat him fair and square in Hungary...

The gap between them was 2.2s after one lap before

THE THRILLS ARE ALIVE

TIMES CHANGE, BUT COULD YOU IMAGINE F1 without Spa?

The future of the famous Belgian track was a dominant theme throughout race weekend. The local stance against tobacco advertising could be an issue in 2003 but there is more to it than that. Money, as ever, is at the root. As a generator of revenue, Spa lies pretty close to the bottom of the pile. With Bahrain, Turkey, China and Russia waiting in the wings with plans for state-of-the-art facilities, Spa could be on borrowed time.

The modern breed of circuit has advantages, for sure. Designer Hermann Tilke thought hard about the new Hockenheim, to make sure there were overtaking opportunities, for example. And spectators are often afforded a better view.

Point is: are they seeing what they want to see? Do they want F1 cars constrained by a plethora of slow-speed corners? Or does F1 need Spa-Francorchamps?

"This place reminds you that you are a racing driver," said Toyota star Allan McNish. "Places like Eau Rouge (above), Blanchimont and Stavelot are all commitment comers. They're why you wanted to do this job in the first place."

Jacques Villeneuve has always loved Spa, too. His need to prove he can take Eau Rouge flat in qualifying led to piles of steaming scrap for both Williams and BAR in years gone by, but the fact he could head off with a telemetry print-out showing he had balls 15mph bigger than his team mate's was justification enough...

This year JV was disappointed, however. "With traction control and more tyre grip it's easy flat for everyone," he lamented.

In qualifying, maybe. But not with a race set-up on heavy tanks. McNish tried it once and gave himself quite a fright. And doing it flat a couple of years ago was what teed up Mika Häkkinen for that memorable pass of Michael Schumacher.

Monaco will always survive. Spa must, too.

Michael eased back for a few laps so as not to blister his softer Bridgestones. Then he trod on it once again and started to go away at a second a lap. He loved the balance of the car from first thing Friday, whereas Rubens had gone for the harder Bridgestone and found it to be the wrong choice.

"But still," Rubens said. "I was better off than our opposition, so I was just able to drive home. Michael was in a different league. It would have been too much to ask for us to change positions. In any case, my rivals were behind me."

Even Ferrari technical director Ross Brawn was a little puzzled as to why Michael was going so fast up front.

"Our immediate feeling was that other people were on a one-stop strategy so we had to keep the pace up," he said. "I kept telling Michael to slow down when the strategies became clearer, but you can see how he responded!"

BRONZE MEDDLE: Olivier Panis and his crew debate where that tan came from, because you don't get to look like this by living in Belgium

THIS WASN'T ONE OF RALF'S BETTER AFTERNOONS. LEAVING THE PITS AFTER HIS SECOND STOP HE PUSHED THE WRONG STEERING WHEEL BUTTON AND STRUGGLED TO GET GOING

Kimi Räikkönen was mighty in Belgium and his total commitment in qualifying gave him a first front-row start. But any thoughts he had of challenging Michael were optimistic. When Barrichello got his Ferrari down the inside of the McLaren at La Source on lap one, it was more a question of whether Kimi could hold onto the second Ferrari.

He tried hard but a lurid slide through Pouhon on lap two let Juan Pablo Montoya through as Kimi sorted himself out.

Montoya drove a fine race. He kept Räikkönen behind him during the first stint and later repelled David Coulthard – who used a more amenable Michelin race tyre than Räikkönen and leap-frogged his team-mate at the first round of stops.

Räikkönen would have finished fifth but his Mercedes V10 expired with nine laps to go and it was left to Ralf Schumacher, more than half a minute behind Coulthard, to claim the two points.

This wasn't one of Ralf's better afternoons. He lost out to Coulthard during the opening-lap run up from Eau Rouge to Les Combes, evidence that Mercedes had found some extra top-end power. Then, under pressure from Jarno Trulli, he spun on his in-lap at the first round of stops and fell back to seventh. Finally, leaving the pits after his second stop, he pushed the wrong steering wheel button and struggled to get going.

Trulli also had an engine failure, which left Eddie Irvine to collect the final point for Jaguar. Having achieved the team's best qualifying performance of the year, Irvine found he could not run with Trulli but managed to hold off Mika Salo's Toyota, which was just 0.4s behind at the flag.

But in an altogether different race Ferrari's total domination had given the team its 50th consecutive podium finish. Or, to put it another way, every grand prix for three years. Stunning, absolutely stunning.

FLASHBACK

June 9 1968, Spa, Belgium

BY THE SUMMER OF 1968 THE NAME McLAREN had appeared only three times at the top of a grand prix results sheet – and each time it belonged to driver rather than car.

Kiwi Bruce McLaren was a gifted engineer and a talented racer. Youngest winner of a world championship F1 race (22 years 3 months and 12 days when he triumphed in the inaugural US GP at Sebring in1959), he stayed loyal to Cooper from 1958-1965 but began running his own team as a sideline late in 1964. Work quickly began to pile up and by the start of 1966 Bruce McLaren Motor Racing became his full-time occupation.

His first F1 car made its debut at Monaco that year and by the end of the following season his creations were showing real promise.

In 1968 the team expanded to two cars, for McLaren (above) and compatriot Denny Hulme. Spa was the third race and Denny qualified fifth, one place ahead of Bruce. He led briefly, too, after pace-setters Chris Amon (Ferrari) and John Surtees (Honda) dropped out, but then he skated up an escape road and handed the advantage to Jackie Stewart (Matra). Hulme was recovering fast, however, when a driveshaft let go.

That seemed to be it. Stewart was 30 seconds clear of McLaren as he approached his final lap... but then his Cosworth engine coughed, almost out of fuel. The Scot pitted for a top-up and McLaren sailed through, unaware of the drama. It was only when he got back to the paddock that he realised he'd won.

His first GP win for six years was also to be his last. For the marque he founded, however, it would be the first of 135... and counting.

BRITAIN,S BEST-SELLING SINGLES... WHEN BRUCE McLAREN WRONGLY ASSUMED HE'D FINISHED SECOND	
1 GARY PUCKETT & THE UNION GAP	Young Girl
2 BOBBY GOLDSBORO	Honey
3 ROLLING STONES	Jumping Jack Flash
4 ENGLEBERT HUMPERDINCK	Man Without Love
5 JULIE DRISCOLL	This Wheel's On Fire

September 1 2002
CIRCUIT DE SPA-FRANCORCHAMPS
STAVELOT
CIRCUIT LENGTH:
4.327miles / 6.963km

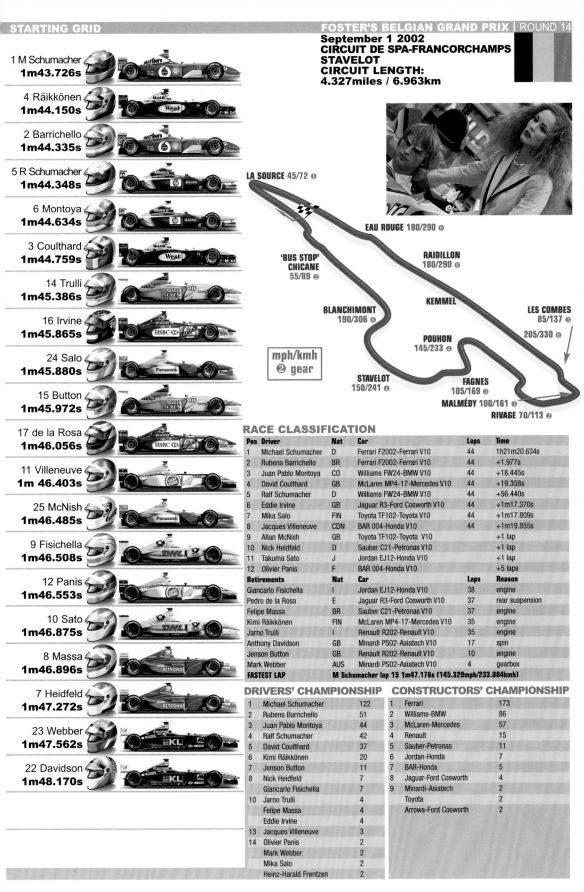

1 M Schumacher
1m43.726s

4 Räikkönen
1m44.150s

2 Barrichello
1m44.335s

5 R Schumacher
1m44.348s

6 Montoya
1m44.634s

3 Coulthard
1m44.759s

14 Trulli
1m45.386s

16 Irvine
1m45.865s

24 Salo
1m45.880s

15 Button
1m45.972s

17 de la Rosa
1m46.056s

11 Villeneuve
1m 46.403s

25 McNish
1m46.485s

9 Fisichella
1m46.508s

12 Panis
1m46.553s

10 Sato
1m46.875s

8 Massa
1m46.896s

7 Heidfeld
1m47.272s

23 Webber
1m47.562s

22 Davidson
1m48.170s

LA SOURCE 45/72 ❶

EAU ROUGE 180/290 ❻

RAIDILLON 180/290 ❻

'BUS STOP' CHICANE 55/89 ❷

KEMMEL

LES COMBES 85/137 ❸

205/330 ❻

BLANCHIMONT 190/306 ❻

POUHON 145/233 ❹

mph/kmh ❷ gear

STAVELOT 150/241 ❹

FAGNES 105/169 ❸

MALMÉDY 100/161 ❺

RIVAGE 70/113 ❷

RACE CLASSIFICATION

Pos	Driver	Nat	Car	Laps	Time
1	Michael Schumacher	D	Ferrari F2002-Ferrari V10	44	1h21m20.634s
2	Rubens Barrichello	BR	Ferrari F2002-Ferrari V10	44	+1.977s
3	Juan Pablo Montoya	CO	Williams FW24-BMW V10	44	+18.445s
4	David Coulthard	GB	McLaren MP4-17-Mercedes V10	44	+19.358s
5	Ralf Schumacher	D	Williams FW24-BMW V10	44	+56.440s
6	Eddie Irvine	GB	Jaguar R3-Ford Cosworth V10	44	+1m17.370s
7	Mika Salo	FIN	Toyota TF102-Toyota V10	44	+1m17.809s
8	Jacques Villeneuve	CDN	BAR 004-Honda V10	44	+1m19.855s
9	Allan McNish	GB	Toyota TF102-Toyota V10		+1 lap
10	Nick Heidfeld	D	Sauber C21-Petronas V10		+1 lap
11	Takuma Sato	J	Jordan EJ12-Honda V10		+1 lap
12	Olivier Panis	F	BAR 004-Honda V10		+5 laps

Retirements	Nat	Car	Laps	Reason
Giancarlo Fisichella	I	Jordan EJ12-Honda V10	38	engine
Pedro de la Rosa	E	Jaguar R3-Ford Cosworth V10	37	rear suspension
Felipe Massa	BR	Sauber C21-Petronas V10	37	engine
Kimi Räikkönen	FIN	McLaren MP4-17-Mercedes V10	35	engine
Jarno Trulli	I	Renault R202-Renault V10	35	engine
Anthony Davidson	GB	Minardi PS02-Asiatech V10	17	spin
Jenson Button	GB	Renault R202-Renault V10	10	engine
Mark Webber	AUS	Minardi PS02-Asiatech V10	4	gearbox

FASTEST LAP M Schumacher lap 15 1m47.176s (145.329mph/233.884kmh)

DRIVERS' CHAMPIONSHIP

1	Michael Schumacher	122
2	Rubens Barrichello	51
3	Juan Pablo Montoya	44
4	Ralf Schumacher	42
5	David Coulthard	37
6	Kimi Räikkönen	20
7	Jenson Button	11
8	Nick Heidfeld	7
	Giancarlo Fisichella	7
10	Jarno Trulli	4
	Felipe Massa	4
	Eddie Irvine	4
13	Jacques Villeneuve	3
14	Olivier Panis	2
	Mark Webber	2
	Mika Salo	2
	Heinz-Harald Frentzen	2

CONSTRUCTORS' CHAMPIONSHIP

1	Ferrari	173
2	Williams-BMW	86
3	McLaren-Mercedes	57
4	Renault	15
5	Sauber-Petronas	11
6	Jordan-Honda	7
7	BAR-Honda	5
8	Jaguar-Ford Cosworth	4
9	Minardi-Asiatech	2
	Toyota	2
	Arrows-Ford Cosworth	2

GRAN PREMIO VODAFONE D'ITALIA

WILLIAMS WAS NO STRANGER TO OUTPACING FERRARI IN QUALIFYING TRIM. THIS WAS JUAN PABLO MONTOYA'S SEVENTH POLE POSITION OF THE YEAR. THERE WAS A BUZZ IN THE PADDOCK: FERRARI MIGHT BE FACING ITS FIRST DEFEAT SINCE MONACO. BUT THEN THE RACE STARTED

GREEN ON RED: Michael became so bored tooling along at Rubens' pace that he lost concentration and almost mowed down the bloke with the flag (above). Left, thousands of Italians wonder what Eddie Irvine is doing on the podium

THE LAWN KING: Ralf led until his engine blew (main shot). For once the Jaguar was a factor rather than a tractor and Irvine (above left) was third on merit. The nearest thing we saw to an Orange Arrows in action all weekend (above right). Below, Massa was the first F1 driver to race with a HANS head-and-neck protector

THE OPTIMISM IN THE WILLIAMS-BMW CAMP LOOKED well placed. Michelin's harder tyre appeared to be as durable as it was fast and Juan Pablo Montoya used it to good effect to set the fastest qualifying lap in Formula One history – 161.484mph, 0.525mph quicker than the benchmark established by Williams-Honda racer Keke Rosberg at Silverstone 17 years beforehand.

When Montoya's launch control faltered momentarily at the start the Colombian didn't hesitate to execute a Schuey-style chop to thwart the move's creator – and that slowed them enough to allow Ralf Schumacher (in the spare Williams, because his own had suffered a dip in fuel pressure) a clean run to the front from third on the grid. At least, it was almost a clean run...

Montoya retained enough momentum to force Ralf wide on the approach to the first chicane, but in doing so he left himself only just enough room to make the corner. Ralf had little option but to leap across the kerbs and into the lead, while Rubens Barrichello – running light on a two-stop fuel load – nipped ahead of Schuey and tagged onto Montoya's tail.

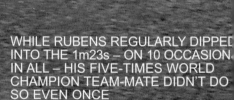

WHILE RUBENS REGULARLY DIPPED INTO THE 1m23s – ON 10 OCCASIONS IN ALL – HIS FIVE-TIMES WORLD CHAMPION TEAM-MATE DIDN'T DO SO EVEN ONCE

On lap three the stewards served notice that Ralf ought to back off and let Montoya through if he wanted to avoid being penalised for taking a short-cut, but it was immaterial because his BMW V10 went bang just as he was preparing to cede. In qualifying trim the BMWs had registered a record-breaking 19,050rpm. In milder race tune, ironically, a pneumatic valve problem caused Ralf's to expire.

As he pulled off in a cloud of steam Barrichello tucked in behind Montoya and slammed into the lead before they reached the braking zone for the first chicane. Montoya's efforts to keep up led to him running wide soon afterwards and the Ferraris were suddenly first and second. An aura of rapture swept over the partisan crowd; a sense of inevitability swamped everybody else.

LOOK BACK ON ENGE

BY THE TIME FORMULA One reached Monza the F1 title contest had been settled for almost two months.

The destiny of the FIA Formula 3000 Championship, however, remained in the balance until the final lap of the season. And beyond...

Frenchman Sébastien Bourdais (Super Nova) arrived with a one-point series lead, but qualified only seventh.

His closest challenger Tomas Enge (Arden International, above) turned up looking weary. Five days beforehand he learned that a random drug test taken two races earlier in Hungary had shown up cannabis in his bloodstream. He denied having knowingly taken any banned substance but its mere presence constituted an offence and he hadn't slept since the news broke. He lined up third, a good effort.

Giorgio Pantano (Coloni) was the outsider: he had to win to have any chance, but even that might not be enough. He started second.

While Enge's team-mate Björn Wirdheim led from pole and did an admirable job fending off Pantano's constant pressure, the Czech loitered in the lower reaches of the top six before moving up to fourth. Bourdais dropped to ninth initially but was up to fifth and closing when his rotor arm snapped. Game over, for now.

A late Safety Car period set up a one-lap sprint to the finish and handed Pantano a gilt-edged chance to nick the main prize. Wirdheim was more alert at the restart, however, and Pantano's all-or-nothing approach left him prone to attack. He slipped to fourth, behind Antonio Pizzonia (Petrobras Jnr) and Enge.

After the race Coloni protested the top three cars on technical grounds and Pizzonia was eventually kicked out for an alleged, but dubious, rear wing infringement. More significantly, more than two weeks after flagfall Enge was stripped of the 10 points he won in Hungary and Bourdais took the title after all. "It's not the best way to win," he said. "These things should be settled on the track."

Enge said: "I am extremely proud of the way I have driven this year and nobody can take that away."

He maintained his dignity in difficult circumstances; the FIA let him keep his racing licence.

Ferrari insisted later that its drivers were racing. Computer simulations showed that one- or two-stop strategies were viable. But while Rubens regularly dipped into the 1m23s – on 10 occasions, in all – his five-times world champion team-mate didn't do so even once. When Michael led the race, between Barrichello's two stops and just before his own, he was ambling along in the low to mid 1m24s, just fast (or slow) enough to ensure that he was right behind his team-mate after Rubens' second and final stop. This was while running on a low fuel load at a track that does not cane tyres significantly. Schuey more than half a second adrift in terms of race pace? You work it out.

"Rubens just drove faster than me today," Michael said later. Perfectly true, but it also looked as though the Brazilian had been trying a trifle harder... The upshot was that Rubens had almost clinched second place in the championship.

Of the rest, Montoya's chances of taking third sagged along with his suspension after an unusual chassis failure. The McLarens touched at the first corner: Kimi Räikkönen emerged unscathed but had his

KERB CALLING:
the Williams twins made
a porridge of the first
chicane (above) but still
managed to keep the
Ferraris at bay for a bit
longer. Right, Räikkönen
checks out the latest
So Solid Crew album on
his Walkman but it fails
to cheer him up

AFTER SIDE-SWIPING DE LA ROSA'S JAGUAR AT 200-ODD MPH, A PENALTY WAS NO MORE THAN MASSA DESERVED

engine blow on lap 30; David Coulthard pitted for a new nose and finished seventh.

That left 250/1 shot Eddie Irvine to breeze home a distant third for much-improved Jaguar. The Ulsterman qualified sixth and lined up fifth after Räikkönen was punished for shoving Takuma Sato's Jordan off the track. In the race he didn't have the McLarens' pace, but he had reliability. "To stand on the podium felt great," he said, "particularly here, where they know how to celebrate properly."

The Renaults of Jarno Trulli and Jenson Button were next – and this was a much improved effort from the under-fire Trulli, who started dead last after his launch control system left him stranded on the grid at the beginning of the final parade lap.

Olivier Panis made good use of a well-drilled two-stopper to claim the final point for BAR, but Toyota went away feeling bitterly disappointed. Allan McNish ran behind Irvine in the early stages, but a front suspension problem ended any chance of breaking his F1 points duck. Mika Salo was comfortably ahead of the Renaults when he crossed the pit exit blend line after a scheduled stop and collected a drive-through penalty that dropped him from fourth to 11th.

Finally, Felipe Massa notched up a couple of landmarks during the weekend. He became the first driver to wear a HANS head-and-neck protection device during a grand prix, and also the first to be docked 10 places on the grid for the next event. After side-swiping Pedro de la Rosa's Jaguar at 200-odd mph it was no more than he deserved.

FLASHBACK
September 5 1971, Monza, Italy

HAD FERRARI TRIED A TOUCH HARDER, THE 2002 Italian GP could have been the fastest in history. After Rubens and Schuey entered cruise mode, however, they failed by 0.949mph to match an event that took place 31 years earlier.

This was the final season before Monza became festooned with chicanes. Chris Amon qualified his Matra MS120B on pole and was in the thick of the lead battle for most of the afternoon. With nine laps to go, however, he adjusted his visor and it flew off. He faded to sixth.

From 11th on the grid Peter Gethin (BRM P160) initially ran with the slipstreaming lead pack, but he lost touch after being baulked while lapping Jean-Pierre Jarier's March. That proved to be a blessing, because his V12 had been running hot in traffic. Once he was on his own, it began to cool and he edged closer to the leaders once more.

At the start of the final lap Ronnie Peterson (March 711) led from François Cevert (Tyrrell 002), Mike Hailwood (Surtees TS9, doing a brilliant job in his first GP since Monaco 1965) and the BRMs of Gethin and Howden Ganley.

Gethin (second left, above) zapped past Hailwood and into third on the back straight. Coming into Parabolica, the final corner, he could see Cevert and Peterson braking deep and late. Peterson's car began to teeter and run wide, forcing Cevert to opt for a tighter line – except that Gethin had already grabbed that. With more momentum out of the corner than Peterson, he went from third to first in a blink.

The Swede hit back, dived into the BRM's slipstream and ducked out on the run to the line, hoping to be sucked past. He fell two feet short. Gethin averaged 150.755mph and won by 0.01s: the fastest-ever GP and also the closest.

BRITAIN'S BEST-SELLING SINGLES... WHEN 0.61s COVERED THE TOP FIVE CARS AT MONZA	
1 THE TAMS	Hey Girl, Don't Bother Me
2 DIANA ROSS	I'm Still Waiting
3 NEW SEEKERS	Never Ending Song Of Love
4 NANCY SINATRA/LEE HAZLEWOOD	Did You Ever
5 DAWN	What Are You Doing Sunday?

September 15 2002
AUTODROMO NAZIONALE DI MONZA,
NEAR MILAN
CIRCUIT LENGTH: 3.600miles / 5.793km

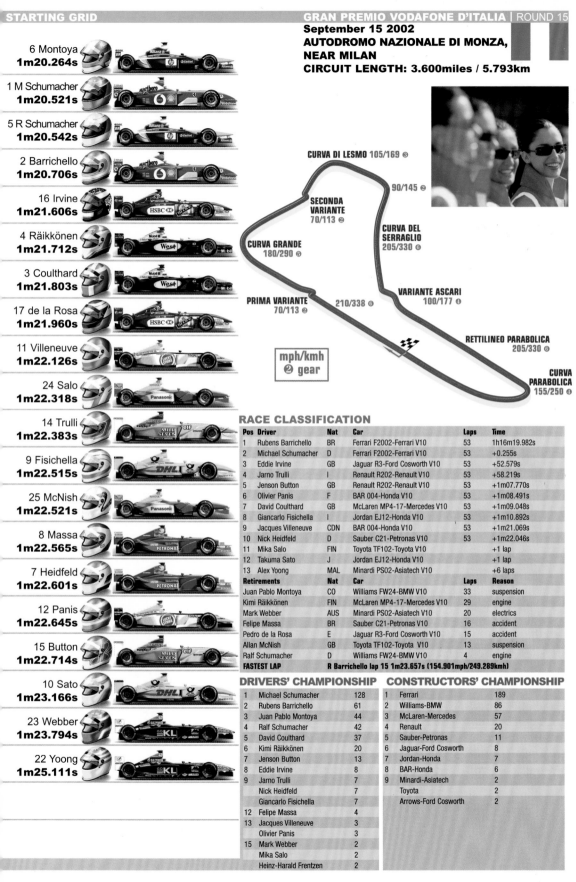

6 Montoya
1m20.264s

1 M Schumacher
1m20.521s

5 R Schumacher
1m20.542s

2 Barrichello
1m20.706s

16 Irvine
1m21.606s

4 Räikkönen
1m21.712s

3 Coulthard
1m21.803s

17 de la Rosa
1m21.960s

11 Villeneuve
1m22.126s

24 Salo
1m22.318s

14 Trulli
1m22.383s

9 Fisichella
1m22.515s

25 McNish
1m22.521s

8 Massa
1m22.565s

7 Heidfeld
1m22.601s

12 Panis
1m22.645s

15 Button
1m22.714s

10 Sato
1m23.166s

23 Webber
1m23.794s

22 Yoong
1m25.111s

CURVA DI LESMO 105/169 ④

90/145 ②

SECONDA
VARIANTE
70/113 ②

CURVA DEL
SERRAGLIO
205/330 ⑥

CURVA GRANDE
180/290 ⑤

PRIMA VARIANTE
70/113 ②

210/338 ⑥

VARIANTE ASCARI
100/177 ①

mph/kmh
❷ gear

RETTILINEO PARABOLICA
205/330 ⑥

CURVA
PARABOLICA
155/250 ①

RACE CLASSIFICATION

Pos	Driver	Nat	Car	Laps	Time
1	Rubens Barrichello	BR	Ferrari F2002-Ferrari V10	53	1h16m19.982s
2	Michael Schumacher	D	Ferrari F2002-Ferrari V10	53	+0.255s
3	Eddie Irvine	GB	Jaguar R3-Ford Cosworth V10	53	+52.579s
4	Jarno Trulli	I	Renault R202-Renault V10	53	+58.219s
5	Jenson Button	GB	Renault R202-Renault V10	53	+1m07.770s
6	Olivier Panis	F	BAR 004-Honda V10	53	+1m08.491s
7	David Coulthard	GB	McLaren MP4-17-Mercedes V10	53	+1m09.048s
8	Giancarlo Fisichella	I	Jordan EJ12-Honda V10	53	+1m10.892s
9	Jacques Villeneuve	CDN	BAR 004-Honda V10	53	+1m21.069s
10	Nick Heidfeld	D	Sauber C21-Petronas V10	53	+1m22.046s
11	Mika Salo	FIN	Toyota TF102-Toyota V10		+1 lap
12	Takuma Sato	J	Jordan EJ12-Honda V10		+1 lap
13	Alex Yoong	MAL	Minardi PS02-Asiatech V10		+6 laps
Retirements		**Nat**	**Car**	**Laps**	**Reason**
	Juan Pablo Montoya	CO	Williams FW24-BMW V10	33	suspension
	Kimi Räikkönen	FIN	McLaren MP4-17-Mercedes V10	29	engine
	Mark Webber	AUS	Minardi PS02-Asiatech V10	20	electrics
	Felipe Massa	BR	Sauber C21-Petronas V10	16	accident
	Pedro de la Rosa	E	Jaguar R3-Ford Cosworth V10	15	accident
	Allan McNish	GB	Toyota TF102-Toyota V10	13	suspension
	Ralf Schumacher	D	Williams FW24-BMW V10	4	engine
FASTEST LAP			**R Barrichello lap 15 1m23.657s (154.901mph/249.289kmh)**		

DRIVERS' CHAMPIONSHIP

1	Michael Schumacher	128
2	Rubens Barrichello	61
3	Juan Pablo Montoya	44
4	Ralf Schumacher	42
5	David Coulthard	37
6	Kimi Räikkönen	20
7	Jenson Button	13
8	Eddie Irvine	8
9	Jarno Trulli	7
	Nick Heidfeld	7
	Giancarlo Fisichella	7
12	Felipe Massa	4
13	Jacques Villeneuve	3
	Olivier Panis	3
15	Mark Webber	2
	Mika Salo	2
	Heinz-Harald Frentzen	2

CONSTRUCTORS' CHAMPIONSHIP

1	Ferrari	189
2	Williams-BMW	86
3	McLaren-Mercedes	57
4	Renault	20
5	Sauber-Petronas	11
6	Jaguar-Ford Cosworth	8
7	Jordan-Honda	7
8	BAR-Honda	6
9	Minardi-Asiatech	2
	Toyota	2
	Arrows-Ford Cosworth	2

SAP UNITED STATES GRAND PRIX

HOW MANY MISTAKES DID MICHAEL SCHUMACHER MAKE IN 2002? SOME PEOPLE FELT HIS TASTE IN SHOES WAS SLIGHTLY FLAWED, BUT ON THE TRACK THERE WERE ONLY A COUPLE OF SMALL BLIPS. THEY WERE QUITE SIGNIFICANT, THOUGH

BRAWN IN THE USA: the SAP girls looked very nice in their Bacofoil but could do with toning their arms. It took two of them to hold a grid board (below). Oi! McLaren bloke! You appear to be looking entirely the wrong way. Oh yes, almost forgot to mention that Ferrari won (left)

INDIANA MO... the Ferraris cross the line as one... but for the sake of 0.011s in favour of Barrichello (main shot, left). Above left, the Ralf Schumacher guide to putting Patrick Head in a steaming rage. Right, bald eagle's-eye view of the start. Far right, Fox Mulder from the X-Files replaced Felipe Massa at Sauber. Below, Kimi rues crunching his McLaren during free practice while a marshal radios in to report a flock of meadow pipits attacking the infield at Turn 11

FERRARI'S JEAN TODT CAME OUT ONE OF THE SEASON'S MOST GUSHING PIECES OF PAP. "THE HAPPINESS OF OUR DRIVERS ON THE PODIUM DEMONSTRATES THE HARMONY THAT EXISTS IN THIS TEAM," HE SAID

THE UNITED STATES IS AN IMPORTANT MARKET FOR Ferrari and its sister company Maserati. The point was drilled home on race morning, when Michael Schumacher demonstrated the Boyle Special Maserati that Wilbur Shaw drove to victory in the 1939 and 1940 Indy 500s.

It was partly a treat for fans, partly slick corporate know-how. Ferrari road cars sell without the need for lavish marketing, but there is never any harm wooing one of your strongest customer bases. Shame, then, that Ferrari left America having alienated the nation's small but loyal Formula One corps.

Everything had gone so smoothly until the race's final few moments. Schuey annexed pole, a couple of tenths clear of Rubens Barrichello, and the Ferraris did their customary vanishing act. But this weekend they raced unfettered. As far as clinching second place in the world championship was concerned, it didn't much matter to Rubens whether he won at Indy or finished behind Michael. He certainly wasn't going to finish behind anyone else.

The two of them went at it hammer and tongs. Michael always held the upper hand, but not by much, and he emerged fractionally ahead after their second and final fuel stops. Still they maintained their relentless pace, circulating comfortably in the high 1m12s and low 1m13s until there were just a couple of laps to go: few cars managed to get anywhere near that kind of pace.

Then, as they breezed into the banked Turn 13 for the final time, Michael eased up. Barrichello swept alongside and the two of them crossed the line almost as one. Almost, because the ultra-sensitive electronic timing system registered that Barrichello was 0.011s ahead.

Afterwards the Ferrari PR machine went into overdrive. "The end of the race wasn't planned like that," Schumacher said. "We tried to cross the line together but failed by a tiny bit." Sporting director Jean Todt came out one of the season's most gushing pieces of pap. "The

FISHER PACED

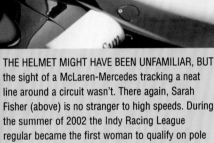

THE HELMET MIGHT HAVE BEEN UNFAMILIAR, BUT the sight of a McLaren-Mercedes tracking a neat line around a circuit wasn't. There again, Sarah Fisher (above) is no stranger to high speeds. During the summer of 2002 the Indy Racing League regular became the first woman to qualify on pole position for a major single-seater race when she lapped Kentucky Motor Speedway at 221.390mph.

At Indy she became the first for more than 10 years to have driven a contemporary Formula One car when she completed a brief demonstration in Kimi Räikkönen's spare chassis.

Her one flying lap wasn't especially quick, but that was irrelevant. She wasn't there to set a time. Rather, this was useful publicity for her, McLaren, her personal sponsor TAG Heuer and the race itself.

Only two women have started world championship grands prix – Maria Teresa de Filippis (in 1958) and Lella Lombardi (in 1975 and 1976). Divina Galica, Desiré Wilson and Giovanna Amati all tried but failed to qualify for races, although Wilson finished sixth for Tyrrell in the 1981 South African GP, which was subsequently stripped of its world championship status. Officially, Lombardi's sixth place for March in the accident-shortened 1975 Spanish GP is the best result any of them achieved.

Fisher's immediate goal is to succeed in the Indy Racing League and to become the first woman to win the Indianapolis 500, the nation's most famous motor sport event. She has not, however, ruled out an eventual switch to F1 – albeit on her terms. "If I was given time to prepare properly I could certainly handle it," she said, "but I'm not interested in doing F1 for F1's sake. It would have to be a competitive proposition. I have been racing since I was five and I'm in this sport to win."

Her IRL rivals have noticed. She has led three races and finished on the podium twice. "It's nice," she said, with a giggle. "They don't look down on me. They know mine is just another fast car they have to beat."

happiness of our drivers on the podium demonstrates the harmony that exists in this team, which works with passion and determination," he said. "That the United States is the most important market for Ferrari and Maserati adds to our satisfaction."

Perhaps he didn't hear the crowd jeering, or read any of the following morning's papers. Some of those that bothered to cover the race suggested Schumacher's actions were the equivalent of a boxer taking a dive to throw a bout.

Except that it wasn't. In public he spoke with reasonable conviction about how Rubens deserved this win, for all the team spirit he had shown earlier in the season. Privately, though, he was angry that he had chucked away victory. His plan had been for the cars to cross the line together, but he had not intended Rubens to be ahead. Like his spin at the Nürburgring seven races earlier, it was a simple, uncharacteristic misjudgement.

THIRD MAN: Coulthard ran the Ferraris closest and scored his sixth podium finish of the year. The following Trulli was on form again, too

DAVID COULTHARD AND McLAREN WERE BEST OF THE REST, ALTHOUGH THE SCOT WAS AIDED BY THE FACT THAT BOTH WILLIAMS DRIVERS APPEARED TO ENGAGE THE SELF-DESTRUCT BUTTON

David Coulthard and McLaren were best of the rest, although the Scot was aided by the fact that both Williams drivers appeared to engage the self-destruct button at about the same time as they primed their launch control.

Coulthard qualified third, immediately ahead of Juan Pablo Montoya and Ralf Schumacher, and beat them off the line. Schuey Jnr moved away most smartly of the Williams pair, but they were side-by-side at the end of the opening lap with Montoya gunning down the outside. He turned into the first corner late, but would have made it through comfortably if Ralf hadn't lost it under braking and spun into him. The team's technical director Patrick Head came perilously close to hitting the pit garage ceiling... and did so again when Montoya, only mildly delayed by the first incident, unexpectedly made his lone pit stop 10 laps before the team was expecting him. Despite everything he finished fourth with a best lap less than 0.1s adrift of the Ferraris. Circumstances had contrived to mask his potential, however. Ralf? He tooled in last, two laps down after stopping for rear wing repairs.

Heinz-Harald Frentzen stood in for Felipe Massa at Sauber, so the Brazilian could escape being penalised 10 places on the grid after his Monza misdemeanours. The German struggled to adapt to a car for which he was six inches too tall, however, and finished 13th.

That was better than Pedro de la Rosa managed. Running an ultra-heavy fuel load, the Spaniard spent 20 laps at the tail of the field before he could squeeze past Alex Yoong's Minardi. A transmission fluid leak then caused the rear end of the R3 to go up in flames, whereupon Pedro hopped out, vaulted the Armco... and landed directly in a stream.

FLASHBACK
March 11 1990, Phoenix, United States

AYRTON SENNA, McLAREN AND HONDA WERE AT the peak of their powers.

The Brazilian had gained the upper hand after two seasons of internal struggle within the team and his nemesis Alain Prost had scarpered to Ferrari. Now McLaren was his fiefdom and, in Gerhard Berger, he had a tame, sociable number two.

In qualifying for 1990's opening race, however, Berger took pole while engine problems restricted Senna to fifth – the first time since Silverstone 1988 that he had not been on the front row.

That was almost as unexpected as the presence of Pier-Luigi Martini's nimble Minardi alongside Berger, or Jean Alesi lining up fourth in the lightweight Tyrrell 018. Both benefited from Pirelli's super-sticky qualifiers.

It might have been Alesi's first full F1 season, but he stormed into the lead at the start (above) while Senna gradually picked his way through the field.

Third by lap five, he took second on lap nine when Berger snagged throttle instead of brake and spun. The road ahead was clear, but Alesi was a couple of seconds to the good. As the McLaren's fuel load lightened Senna moved closer, but the Frenchman was quick and tidy. This would be no pushover.

On lap 34 Senna dived for the inside at Turn One. He was through, but only for a second. Alesi hit back and muscled Senna aside. It took another lap before Ayrton made a move stick. Caught the Brazilian's attention, that. Several teams noticed, too. Ferrari later won the fight for Alesi's signature, but it was not a good time to be joining... especially when he could have had a Williams-Renault instead.

For all the sparkle he showed at Phoenix, Jean would win only once in 201 GP starts.

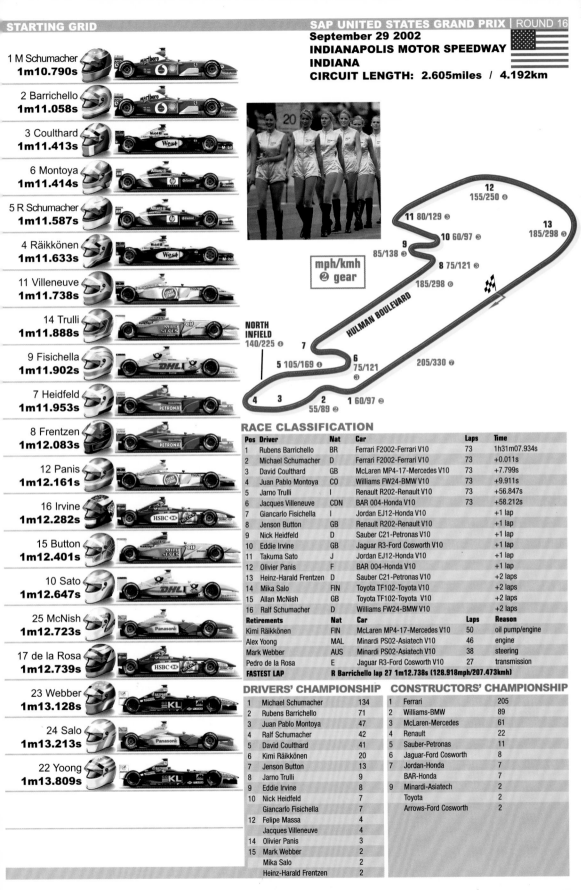

1 M Schumacher
1m10.790s

2 Barrichello
1m11.058s

3 Coulthard
1m11.413s

6 Montoya
1m11.414s

5 R Schumacher
1m11.587s

4 Räikkönen
1m11.633s

11 Villeneuve
1m11.738s

14 Trulli
1m11.888s

9 Fisichella
1m11.902s

7 Heidfeld
1m11.953s

8 Frentzen
1m12.083s

12 Panis
1m12.161s

16 Irvine
1m12.282s

15 Button
1m12.401s

10 Sato
1m12.647s

25 McNish
1m12.723s

17 de la Rosa
1m12.739s

23 Webber
1m13.128s

24 Salo
1m13.213s

22 Yoong
1m13.809s

RACE CLASSIFICATION

Pos	Driver	Nat	Car	Laps	Time
1	Rubens Barrichello	BR	Ferrari F2002-Ferrari V10	73	1h31m07.934s
2	Michael Schumacher	D	Ferrari F2002-Ferrari V10	73	+0.011s
3	David Coulthard	GB	McLaren MP4-17-Mercedes V10	73	+7.799s
4	Juan Pablo Montoya	CO	Williams FW24-BMW V10	73	+9.911s
5	Jarno Trulli	I	Renault R202-Renault V10	73	+56.847s
6	Jacques Villeneuve	CDN	BAR 004-Honda V10	73	+58.212s
7	Giancarlo Fisichella	I	Jordan EJ12-Honda V10		+1 lap
8	Jenson Button	GB	Renault R202-Renault V10		+1 lap
9	Nick Heidfeld	D	Sauber C21-Petronas V10		+1 lap
10	Eddie Irvine	GB	Jaguar R3-Ford Cosworth V10		+1 lap
11	Takuma Sato	J	Jordan EJ12-Honda V10		+1 lap
12	Olivier Panis	F	BAR 004-Honda V10		+1 lap
13	Heinz-Harald Frentzen	D	Sauber C21-Petronas V10		+2 laps
14	Mika Salo	FIN	Toyota TF102-Toyota V10		+2 laps
15	Allan McNish	GB	Toyota TF102-Toyota V10		+2 laps
16	Ralf Schumacher	D	Williams FW24-BMW V10		+2 laps

Retirements	Nat	Car	Laps	Reason
Kimi Räikkönen	FIN	McLaren MP4-17-Mercedes V10	50	oil pump/engine
Alex Yoong	MAL	Minardi PS02-Asiatech V10	46	engine
Mark Webber	AUS	Minardi PS02-Asiatech V10	38	steering
Pedro de la Rosa	E	Jaguar R3-Ford Cosworth V10	27	transmission
FASTEST LAP		**R Barrichello lap 27 1m12.738s (128.918mph/207.473kmh)**		

DRIVERS' CHAMPIONSHIP

1	Michael Schumacher	134
2	Rubens Barrichello	71
3	Juan Pablo Montoya	47
4	Ralf Schumacher	42
5	David Coulthard	41
6	Kimi Räikkönen	20
7	Jenson Button	13
8	Jarno Trulli	9
9	Eddie Irvine	8
10	Nick Heidfeld	7
	Giancarlo Fisichella	7
12	Felipe Massa	4
	Jacques Villeneuve	4
14	Olivier Panis	3
15	Mark Webber	2
	Mika Salo	2
	Heinz-Harald Frentzen	2

CONSTRUCTORS' CHAMPIONSHIP

1	Ferrari	205
2	Williams-BMW	89
3	McLaren-Mercedes	61
4	Renault	22
5	Sauber-Petronas	11
6	Jaguar-Ford Cosworth	8
7	Jordan-Honda	7
	BAR-Honda	7
9	Minardi-Asiatech	2
	Toyota	2
	Arrows-Ford Cosworth	2

FUJI TELEVISION JAPANESE GRAND PRIX

ONE OF THIS BOOK'S TWO AUTHORS BET AGAINST MICHAEL SCHUMACHER AT SUZUKA. AND AS SOON AS HE'D PLACED IT, TONY DODGINS WINCED. HE KNOWS YOU DON'T DO THAT...

MICHAEL WINNER: Schuey increased his record-breaking seasonal victory tally to 11 and Kimi had worked out how to exercise his lip muscles by the season's end (above). As far as the fans were concerned, however, the moral victor was the bloke who finished fifth (left). Sato drove magnificently

THE MICHELIN RUNNERS LOOKED GOOD ON FRIDAY, particularly the two McLarens. Suzuka is similar to Spa in many ways so it was no surprise to see Kimi Räikkönen get stuck in and set the pace. When it mattered, however, there was only ever going to be one outcome in qualifying. The Schuey/Ferrari/Bridgestone triumvirate was unstoppable, his 1m31.317s best fully 1.167s quicker than his pole-annexing lap the previous year. This was his fifth straight pole in Japan. Rubens Barrichello did well to stay within half a second – and David Coulthard put in one of his laps of the season to be vaguely in touch with the Brazilian. It was a bitty, session, though – interrupted for more than an hour because Allan McNish's Toyota vaulted the barriers after the Scot lost control at the exit of 130R. Somehow, implausibly, the only casualties were one Toyota TF102 and a bruised knee (see sidebar, right).

For Coulthard to have had any chance of getting among the Ferraris he needed a dynamite start. His wasn't bad, but Michael's was perfect. At the end of the opening lap he was almost 2.3 seconds clear of Rubens. Job done.

Schuey pulled away as he pleased and backed off at the end for the benefit of a formation finish – this time without unnecessary theatrics.

FAIRGROUND ATTRACTION the yellow rollercoaster (main shot) gives you a decent adrenalin rush when it takes off from base, but the twisty-turny parts are a bit tame. The red one (out of shot) is better. One of the BARs dropped out after someone stuffed a building brick up its exhaust, allegedly (above left). Schuey roars off into the distance while everyone else queues up to file in behind Rubens (below left)

He had become the first man in history to finish on the podium in every round of the world championship (officially 11 wins, five seconds and a third, although really that should have been a 13-3-1 formation) and stretched his records for wins and points in a season to 11 and 144 respectively. With 50 poles under his belt, even the late Ayrton Senna's tally of 65 is likely to crumble. At some stage in 2003 he will become the first driver to have scored 1000 championship points. Only another 55 to go...

In winning 15 races (nine of them one-twos) Ferrari had equalled a record set by McLaren in 1988, although the British team admittedly managed it when there was one fewer race.

Afterwards Michael was gracious in victory. "It's hard to find the words to describe this season," he said. "I think the results speak for themselves." He paused for a moment, then added. "I think this was a good race for the Japanese fans, because they saw two winners today..."

SCHUMACHER HAD BECOME THE FIRST MAN IN HISTORY TO FINISH ON THE PODIUM IN EVERY ROUND OF THE WORLD CHAMPIONSHIP

TOYOTA LAND BRUISER

THE MEDIA ROOM FELL SILENT AND WITHIN moments the sound of engines had stopped, too. Common signals, both, that something dramatic has happened.

On this occasion, however, the hush did not signify fear for a driver's well-being. We had all seen Allan McNish scramble from his wrecked Toyota (above) before he sat down, recovered his thoughts and hobbled away towards a waiting Medical Car. We knew he was all right, but the sheer violence of the impact he had survived (with no more than a bruised right knee, remarkably) still took the breath away.

The Scot's Toyota twitched coming through the 175mph 130R corner, then developed a full-on tankslapper before slewing off to the right. After skimming across the gravel the car slammed backwards into the tyre wall at about 125mph. Momentarily it was subjected to a force estimated at 57g before it rose up, flipped backwards over the guardrail, slammed to earth upside-down and rolled back onto its wheels. Or, rather, the two that were left.

"I didn't have time to be frightened," McNish said. "The car began to oversteer, I put on a bit of opposite lock and then it snapped back the other way. I'm a bit sore but I feel fine and see no reason why I can't race tomorrow."

Having been cleared to take part in the warm-up he lapped 13th fastest and then presented himself to the FIA's medical team for a secondary inspection. This time, however, it was decided that 53 laps might not be a wise investment for his knee and the Scot was told he would have to watch what would otherwise have been his final GP for Toyota.

"It's a massive disappointment," he said, "because when I drove in the warm-up I felt absolutely fine, but I have to respect medical opinion."

He qualified 18th on the grid and would have had precious little to race for, but his passion to compete was absolute. Given what he had just been through, the doctors weren't the only people who deserved respect.

NO SMOKE WITHOUT TYRE: Räikkönen pushing on with above average vigour as he heads for his fourth podium finish of the season and sixth place in the world championship

SATO GAINED A PLACE WHEN RALF SCHUMACHER'S WILLIAMS CROAKED TO A HALT WITH FOUR LAPS TO RUN. THE PLACE WENT BONKERS, THE CHEERS ABOUT DOUBLE THE VOLUME THAT ACCOMPANY A SCHUEY SUCCESS IN GERMANY

The other one? Takuma Sato.

After a trying debut season, this was a magnificent finale for the Jordan-Honda star, whose presence in F1 caused TV viewing figures in Japan to go up by something like 30 per cent. He had suffered more than his fair share of bad luck – and it looked to have struck again when he suffered an engine failure on Saturday morning. The latest-spec Honda V10 held together in the afternoon, however, and he qualified a best-ever seventh.

He held station in the early stages of the race, when his car felt slightly out of balance, and was jumped by the Renaults of Jarno Trulli and Jenson Button at the first of two stops. The team used the pause to give Taku a little more front wing and, balance restored, he emerged ahead of Button after refuelling for the second time. With Trulli having just retired because of an engine problem, Sato was up to sixth but he gained a position when Ralf Schumacher's third-placed Williams croaked to a halt with four laps to run. The place went bonkers, the cheers about double the volume that accompany a Schuey success in Germany.

"This is an incredible feeling," Sato said, with a beam. "It's one of the best I have known. The fans were unbelievable. I was aware of them cheering and waving from start to finish." It was a faultless drive – one of the best by anybody all season.

The rest? Coulthard ran third early on but was soon out with throttle system failure. Räikkönen inherited the place, however, after Schuey Jnr's late demise. Montoya looked like he was enjoying himself in the theme park on Thursday evening, but struggled all weekend to balance his Williams and trailed in fourth.

It was a characteristic Ferrari performance that typified the way the season had gone. "We are refocusing our efforts," said McLaren boss Ron Dennis, "and I believe we will be much more competitive in 2003. But I'm under no illusions. So will Ferrari."

Teams filtered away in the knowledge that Michael had not suffered a mechanical breakdown during a race for 15 months.

FLASHBACK
October 24 1976, Fuji, Japan

IT WAS ONE OF THE MOST DRAMATIC championship finales F1 has ever known. James Hunt (above) versus Niki Lauda. English public schoolboy against the man who less than three months earlier had been read the last rites following his violent accident at the Nürburgring.

Somehow, Lauda had missed only two races post-Germany. Hunt, meanwhile, had closed to within three points of the Austrian. It was headline news. At a time when the sport was generally ignored by British TV, the BBC and ITV both showed recorded highlights.

On race morning it tipped down. The start was delayed. Several drivers – Hunt included – initially said they wouldn't take part, but eventually they did. After a couple of laps Lauda pulled in. In recent months he had come to appreciate the value of life and such fresh perspective persuaded him there were better ways of spending sodden Sunday afternoons. Several others followed his lead.

Hunt led from the start and, with Lauda gone, needed to finish only third. But in the closing stages of the race the track was drying – and quickly. Hunt's Goodyears were beginning to fall apart. He slipped to third, behind Mario Andretti's Lotus and Patrick Depailler's Tyrrell, but then the Frenchman suffered a blown tyre. Hunt was second again, and safe... Then, with five laps to go, his left front shredded. He clattered into the pits for fresh rubber and rejoined in fifth.

Two laps to go. Hunt scythes past Clay Regazzoni (Ferrari) and Alan Jones (Surtees). Third. Trouble is, he doesn't know. On exiting the car he immediately berates the team for not bringing him in before his tyre blew. It takes a few moments for the good news to percolate.

BRITAIN'S BEST-SELLING SINGLES... WHEN JAMES HUNT DIDN'T REALISE HE WAS WORLD CHAMPION	
1 PUSSYCAT	Mississippi
2 ABBA	Dancing Queen
3 ROD STEWART	Sailing
4 REAL THING	Can't Get By Without You
5 DEMIS ROUSSOS	When Forever Has Gone

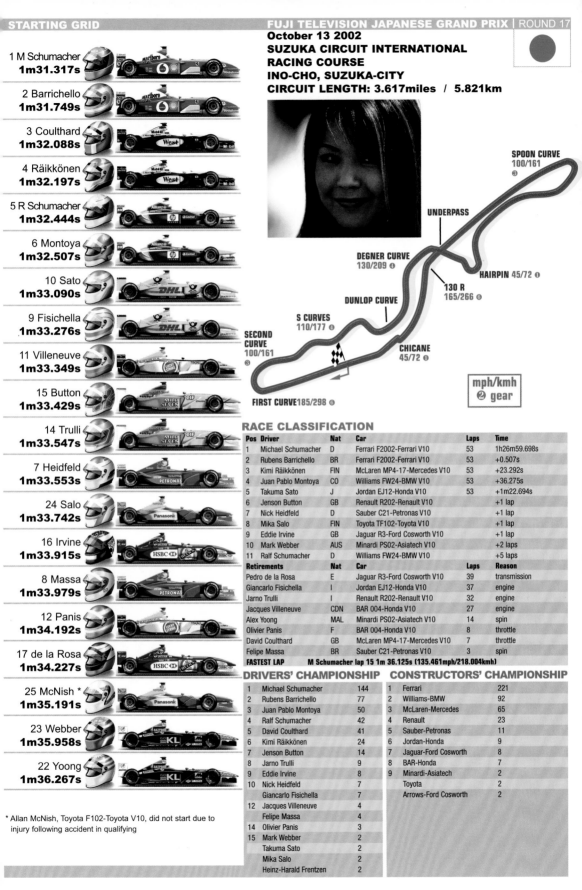

Starting Grid

1 M Schumacher **1m31.317s**
2 Barrichello **1m31.749s**
3 Coulthard **1m32.088s**
4 Räikkönen **1m32.197s**
5 R Schumacher **1m32.444s**
6 Montoya **1m32.507s**
10 Sato **1m33.090s**
9 Fisichella **1m33.276s**
11 Villeneuve **1m33.349s**
15 Button **1m33.429s**
14 Trulli **1m33.547s**
7 Heidfeld **1m33.553s**
24 Salo **1m33.742s**
16 Irvine **1m33.915s**
8 Massa **1m33.979s**
12 Panis **1m34.192s**
17 de la Rosa **1m34.227s**
25 McNish * **1m35.191s**
23 Webber **1m35.958s**
22 Yoong **1m36.267s**

* Allan McNish, Toyota F102-Toyota V10, did not start due to injury following accident in qualifying

Circuit Map

SPOON CURVE 100/161 ③
UNDERPASS
DEGNER CURVE 130/209 ①
HAIRPIN 45/72 ①
130 R 165/266 ⑥
DUNLOP CURVE
S CURVES 110/177 ①
SECOND CURVE 100/161 ③
CHICANE 45/72 ①
FIRST CURVE 185/298 ⑥

mph/kmh ② gear

RACE CLASSIFICATION

Pos	Driver	Nat	Car	Laps	Time
1	Michael Schumacher	D	Ferrari F2002-Ferrari V10	53	1h26m59.698s
2	Rubens Barrichello	BR	Ferrari F2002-Ferrari V10	53	+0.507s
3	Kimi Räikkönen	FIN	McLaren MP4-17-Mercedes V10	53	+23.292s
4	Juan Pablo Montoya	CO	Williams FW24-BMW V10	53	+36.275s
5	Takuma Sato	J	Jordan EJ12-Honda V10	53	+1m22.694s
6	Jenson Button	GB	Renault R202-Renault V10		+1 lap
7	Nick Heidfeld	D	Sauber C21-Petronas V10		+1 lap
8	Mika Salo	FIN	Toyota TF102-Toyota V10		+1 lap
9	Eddie Irvine	GB	Jaguar R3-Ford Cosworth V10		+1 lap
10	Mark Webber	AUS	Minardi PS02-Asiatech V10		+2 laps
11	Ralf Schumacher	D	Williams FW24-BMW V10		+5 laps

Retirements	Nat	Car	Laps	Reason
Pedro de la Rosa	E	Jaguar R3-Ford Cosworth V10	39	transmission
Giancarlo Fisichella	I	Jordan EJ12-Honda V10	37	engine
Jarno Trulli	I	Renault R202-Renault V10	32	engine
Jacques Villeneuve	CDN	BAR 004-Honda V10	27	engine
Alex Yoong	MAL	Minardi PS02-Asiatech V10	14	spin
Olivier Panis	F	BAR 004-Honda V10	8	throttle
David Coulthard	GB	McLaren MP4-17-Mercedes V10	7	throttle
Felipe Massa	BR	Sauber C21-Petronas V10	3	spin

FASTEST LAP M Schumacher lap 15 1m 36.125s (135.461mph/218.004kmh)

DRIVERS' CHAMPIONSHIP

1	Michael Schumacher	144
2	Rubens Barrichello	77
3	Juan Pablo Montoya	50
4	Ralf Schumacher	42
5	David Coulthard	41
6	Kimi Räikkönen	24
7	Jenson Button	14
8	Jarno Trulli	9
9	Eddie Irvine	8
10	Nick Heidfeld	7
	Giancarlo Fisichella	7
12	Jacques Villeneuve	4
	Felipe Massa	4
14	Olivier Panis	3
15	Mark Webber	2
	Takuma Sato	2
	Mika Salo	2
	Heinz-Harald Frentzen	2

CONSTRUCTORS' CHAMPIONSHIP

1	Ferrari	221
2	Williams-BMW	92
3	McLaren-Mercedes	65
4	Renault	23
5	Sauber-Petronas	11
6	Jordan-Honda	9
7	Jaguar-Ford Cosworth	8
8	BAR-Honda	7
9	Minardi-Asiatech	2
	Toyota	2
	Arrows-Ford Cosworth	2

THIS IS BEING WRITTEN BETWEEN JAPAN AND England, aboard a KLM Boeing 747 on which the bloke ahead has reclined his chair so far that my laptop is more or less bent double. I had back-of-the-chair-against-knee syndrome all the way to Australia in March, too, except that I didn't get my computer out then because Singapore Airlines had individual arcade game-equipped video screens for each seat and it was a chance to relive the Eighties for 20-odd hours. Wake up, KLM.

Point is, that marathon Super Mario session feels like it happened barely a couple of weeks ago. Ferrari's dominance is supposed to have rendered the sport a trifle dull. If you happened to be there, however, the 17 races passed in the blink of an eye. In future, perhaps, we'll sit there with a nip of malt and say, "Wow, remember how good Ferrari was when..."

The downside is that Ferrari has pretty much been treating the sport as its own personal playground – and that is a direct result of rivals' persistent failure to match the Italian team's standards. The manner in which it stage-managed the finish in Austria was gauche. It was a business decision, no more, no less. Paying punters and TV viewers still regard this as a sport, however, hence the outcry. If you were watching closely you'd have struggled to see any real racing at Monza, either, but the *trompe l'oeil* was more effective and thus did not upset viewers'

sensibilities. Indianapolis? A cock-up that didn't exactly help promote the sport's image in the United States.

Ferrari has been able to control events thanks to long-term continuity with high-class personnel. Some will point at the Scuderia's colossal budget. Fair enough, the team is loaded... but so it was in the early 1990s, when Jean Alesi and Gerhard Berger were at the helm. Didn't notice it winning a huge number of races then.

Since 1996 Ferrari has invested in the leading brains and assembled them around the best driver. It has been an evolutionary process and 2002 provided the most graphic illustration yet of its effectiveness. The team that won no world titles for 15 seasons has now scooped seven in the last four.

At the end of the year there was talk about introducing weight penalties for successful teams, but that would be a primitive solution. It works in some types of motor racing but has no place in F1, where the culture is to push back fresh technical frontiers. Bunging extra weight in the Ferrari would be a bit like telling Arsène Wenger that Thierry Henry must play with his bootlaces tied together on Sunday to give West Brom a fighting chance. Or making Tiger Woods tee off from Carlisle the next time the British Open takes place at St Andrews.

The bottom line? The rest must polish their acts and catch up.

VINTAGE RED

THIS BOOK IS THE TALE OF A ONE-PRANCING HORSE RACE... FERRARI'S DOMINATION IN 2002 MIGHT HAVE EARNED FORMULA ONE AND THE TEAM A LOT OF FLAK, BUT MUCH OF THE CRITICISM WAS MISDIRECTED

Rivals McLaren-Mercedes and Williams-BMW have the technical and financial resources to react immediately. Renault, BAR-Honda, Jaguar and Toyota have major manufacturer support and the potential to succeed, but the future looks more difficult for the rest. Sauber (with its Ferrari-sourced Petronas engines) and Jordan (with customer Ford-Cosworths from 2003) ought to survive, despite the dwindling availability of sponsorship resources. Prost collapsed before a wheel had turned in 2002, however, and Arrows vanished mid-season. Minardi plugged on thanks to the injection of some TV rights money to which it believed it was entitled, but when it was suggested that this might have to be repaid team boss Paul Stoddart's response was curt and clear. "If that happens, Minardi goes bust. Simple."

It has been proposed that the FIA should introduce a number of controlled components that will be mandatory for all teams – electronic management systems, that kind of thing. This would equalise performance to a degree and bring down the cost of competing. There could be no more appropriate time than the present to introduce such measures.

GPY AWARDS 2002•03

TOP 10 DRIVERS

(2001 ratings in brackets)
1 (1) Michael Schumacher(left)
2 (2) Juan Pablo Montoya
3 (7) Kimi Räikkönen
4 (-) Rubens Barrichello
5 (4) David Coulthard
6 (3) Giancarlo Fisichella
7 (-) Jenson Button
8 (-) Mark Webber
9 (-) The trucker who e-mailed Radio 5 Live to rail against striking London Underground tube drivers. "I get paid less than half what they earn," he wrote, "and I have to steer as well."
10 (-) Ralf Schumacher

TOP 5 CARS
1 Ferrari F2002 (main pic)
2 Ferrari F2001
3 Fly's Chevron B19 slot-racer
4 Williams FW24
5 Tamiya's 1/24-scale model of Jody Scheckter's Wolf WR1 (below)

MOST DRUNKEN FANS (2001 ratings in brackets)
1 (3) The Germans at the Nürburgring
2 (-) Half a dozen Japanese businessmen in a hotel lift near Suzuka
3 (-) The Germans in Austria
4 (3) The Germans in Hockenheim
5 (5) The Germans in Belgium

BEST RACE
Monaco (bizarrely)

WORST RACE
Hungary

BIGGEST MISJUDGEMENTS
1 A moped rider tootling along the motorway hard shoulder against oncoming traffic on Saturday morning in Malaysia
2 Takuma Sato turning left in the tunnel at Monaco. Very wrong
3 Michael Schumacher trying to sort out a nice photo-finish at Indianapolis

BEST PERFORMANCES

1 David Coulthard in Monaco
2 Michael Schumacher everywhere
3 Kimi Räikkönen in France
4 Williams technical director Patrick Head breaking the world record for height attained during vertical take-off from a plastic chair after his two clowns collided in Indianapolis
5 Juan Pablo Montoya (above) in qualifying at Monaco and Silverstone
6 Takuma Sato driving his socks off in Japan
7 Brazil in the World Cup

WORST PERFORMANCES

1 Ferrari's corporate attempts to conceal the facts (hello Jean Todt, left)
2 Jarno Trulli in the first 14 races
3 Ralf Schumacher pretty much everywhere
4 Finnish fans failing to turn up and perform their traditional getting-plastered-en-masse routine in Hungary
5 The cast of Friends – can anyone explain the attraction?
6 France in the World Cup

BEST MOVES

1 Juan Pablo Montoya passing Ralf Schumacher and Kimi Räikkönen in one hit, Canada
2 Montoya and Michael Schumacher against each other, several times, in Melbourne
3 Kimi Räikkönen on Montoya in Hungary
4 More or less the whole field passing Jarno Trulli in the space of two corners at Hockenheim

WORST MOVES

1 Spider Man. What? Sorry, thought you said movie
2 Closure of Sam's CD store in Montreal
3 Anything Felipe Massa did between laps one and 11 (approximately) at Silverstone

4 Massa (left) on Pedro de la Rosa at Monza
5 Alex Ribeiro opening the Medical Car door during the Sunday morning warm-up in Brazil
6 Atomic Kitten doing a cover of The Tide Is High

BEST PLACES TO VISIT

Spa (for spectacle) Indianapolis, left (for facilities and jazz bars) Budapest (if you stay in the city centre and keep away from the track), Monaco (for all-round sensory assault), Le Chais (wine store tucked away in the back streets of Calais, handy en route to Hockenheim, the Nürburgring, Spa, Magny-Cours etc etc)

BEST FOOD

1 Italy
2 Italy
3 The Thai restaurant by the Danube in Budapest, Hungary
4 Italian restaurants outside Italy
5 Everywhere else that isn't Austria or Germany. Or Britain, come to that

THE SUNDERLAND FC AWARD FOR LYING DOWN AND HAVING YOUR TUMMY TICKLED (BY EVERYBODY APART FROM ASTON VILLA)

1 Jarno Trulli (supporters club, left)
2 Jarno Trulli
3 Jarno Trulli
4 Ralf Schumacher
5 Jarno Trulli

SAVE OF THE SEASON

Kimi Räikkönen (below), lap two, Pouhon, Spa